Corporate Governance - Evolving Practices and Emerging Challenges

Edited by Tahir Mumtaz Awan

Published in London, United Kingdom

Corporate Governance - Evolving Practices and Emerging Challenges
http://dx.doi.org/10.5772/10.5772/intechopen.1001796
Edited by Tahir Mumtaz Awan

Assistant to the Editor: Zohaib Riaz Pitafi

Contributors
Andre Baptista Barcaui, Carlos Aparicio Puentes, Carmen Pénnanen-Arias, David Álvarez-Maldonado, Khalid Al-Adeem, Marcela Castro, Mohammad Hormozi, Nicolás Barrientos-Oradini, Paula Misan Klajnberg, Tahir Mumtaz Awan, Víctor Manuel Yáñez Jara, Zohaib Riaz Pitafi

First published in London, United Kingdom, 2024 by IntechOpen
IntechOpen is the global imprint of INTECHOPEN LIMITED, registered in England and Wales, registration number: 11086078, 167-169 Great Portland Street, London, W1W 5PF, United Kingdom

British Library Cataloguing-in-Publication Data
A catalogue record for this book is available from the British Library

Additional hard and PDF copies can be obtained from orders@intechopen.com

Corporate Governance - Evolving Practices and Emerging Challenges
Edited by Tahir Mumtaz Awan
p. cm.

This title is part of the Business, Management and Economics Book Series, Volume 21
Topic: Business and Management
Series Editor: Taufiq Choudhry
Topic Editors: Vito Bobek and Tatjana Horvat

Print ISBN 978-0-85466-923-3
Online ISBN 978-0-85466-922-6
eBook (PDF) ISBN 978-0-85466-924-0
ISSN 2753-894X

For EU product safety concerns:
IN TECH d.o.o., Prolaz Marije Krucifikse Kozulić 3, 51000 Rijeka, Croatia,
info@intechopen.com or visit our website at intechopen.com.

IntechOpen Book Series

Business, Management and Economics

Volume 21

Aims and Scope of the Series

This series will provide a comprehensive overview of recent research trends in business and management, economics, and marketing. Topics will include asset liability management, financial consequences of the financial crisis and covid-19, financial accounting, mergers and acquisitions, management accounting, SMEs, financial markets, corporate finance and governance, managerial technology and innovation, resource management and sustainable development, social entrepreneurship, corporate responsibility, ethics and accountability, microeconomics, labour economics, macroeconomics, public economics, financial economics, econometrics, direct marketing, creative marketing, internet marketing, market planning and forecasting, brand management, market segmentation and targeting and other topics under business and management. This book series will focus on various aspects of business and management whose in-depth understanding is critical for business and company management to function effectively during this uncertain time of financial crisis, Covid-19 pandemic, and military activity in Europe.

Meet the Series Editor

Prof. Choudhry holds a BSc degree in Economics from the University of Iowa, as well as a Masters and Ph.D. in Applied Economics from Clemson University, USA. In January 2006, he became a Professor of Finance at the University of Southampton Business School. He was previously a Professor of Finance at the University of Bradford Management School. He has over 80 articles published in international finance and economics journals. His research interests and specialties include financial econometrics, financial economics, international economics and finance, housing markets, financial markets, among others.

Meet the Volume Editor

Dr. Tahir Mumtaz Awan holds a Ph.D. in Marketing from the School of Business, Sun Yat-sen University (中山大学管 理学院), China. He is Head of the China Study Centre and Assistant Professor of Marketing at COMSATS University Islamabad, Pakistan. He is also an adjunct associate professor at the School of Business Sciences, University of the Witwatersrand, South Africa; Senior Research Fellow at the Center of Ethnology and Anthropology, Hunan Normal University, China; and a researcher at the World Sinology Center, Beijing Language and Culture University, China. Dr. Awan also serves the United Nations Development Programme (UNDP) as a National Expert (Pakistan) for the Cross Cutting Practice - National Experts Program. He has trained Executive Master of Business Administration (EMBA) students at the SKOLKOVO Moscow School of Management and is a regular member of the global business exposure visits team of various business schools in China. He was a Youth of Excellence Fellow for one year in the China Studies Program at Zhejiang University, hosted by the Ministry of Education, China. He was also a United Nations Systems Staff College Fellow in Big Data for Sustainable Development. He was awarded research productivity awards by the Higher Education Commission of Pakistan and Common Ground Publishing of the University of Illinois, Urbana Champaign, USA. He was also awarded a scholarship for higher studies by the Higher Education Commission of Pakistan in support of his Ph.D. He delivered multiple talks, training, and keynotes about China's Belt and Road Initiative, the China–Pakistan Economic Corridor, marketing in developing countries, Big Data, cryptocurrencies, and more. He has nearly fifty academic articles and twelve book chapters to his credit. He has also edited five books. He serves on numerous journal editorial boards. Dr. Awan aims to help improve the interpersonal relationships among Asian and South African and Chinese citizens to provide youth with better placement opportunities. To realize this aim, he is currently providing hands-on experience to Pakistani youth in learning about China and helping them land positions in Chinese firms in Pakistan. Similarly, he is working with African universities to bring more collaborative initiatives for Asian and African regions. He also runs a Pak-China Youth Club from the China Study Centre, COMSATS University Islamabad, and is establishing an African Centre for Business Studies at a South African university.

Contents

Preface

This book provides a thorough analysis of the evolving dynamics of corporate governance. The discussions encompass a broad range of issues, reflecting both the enduring foundations and the innovative approaches reshaping contemporary governance across various global contexts. The work begins by exploring the critical interplay between corporate social responsibility and corporate performance, examining trends across several economic sectors and geographic regions. This sets the stage for deeper inquiries into how different regulatory and cultural landscapes influence governance practices. Particular emphasis is placed on the integration of environmental, social, and governance (ESG) factors, which are becoming increasingly significant in shaping corporate policies worldwide. The book also investigates how these practices are implemented in different industries and the emerging challenges that corporations face in adhering to these new standards.

Further, the theme extends to stakeholder engagement and the strategic importance of ethical governance in fostering sustainable business practices. It also touches upon the implications of governance in the digital realm, particularly the ethical management of personal data, which has become a pivotal issue in the digital age. Through a collection of analytical discussions, the book encourages a reflective examination of how foundational governance principles are applied in practice, and whether they serve as a mere advantage or a necessity in promoting transparency and accountability in today's corporate world. Each chapter contributes to a comprehensive understanding of contemporary issues, drawing on a wide array of perspectives to enrich the debate and provide insights into effective governance strategies. *Corporate Governance – Evolving Practices and Emerging Challenges* is designed to be an invaluable resource for those engaged in the study, practice, or teaching of corporate governance, offering a detailed and critical examination of the field's current trends and future directions.

I wish to extend my deepest gratitude to the Assistant to the Editor, Mr. Zohaib R. Pitafi, whose exceptional contributions have been crucial to the completion of this book. Mr. Pitafi has demonstrated remarkable dedication and proficiency in managing editorial tasks, coordinating research efforts, and ensuring the accuracy of content. His meticulous attention to detail, adept handling of correspondence, and support in the logistical aspects of the publication process have significantly enhanced the quality and coherence of this work. Mr. Pitafi's invaluable assistance and commitment have greatly facilitated the successful realization of this book, and his role has been indispensable throughout.

Dr. Tahir Mumtaz Awan
Head,
China Study Centre,

Assistant Professor,
Department of Management Sciences,
COMSATS University Islamabad,
Islamabad, Pakistan

Adjunct Associate Professor,
School of Business Sciences,
University of the Witwatersrand,
Johannesburg, South Africa

Senior Research Fellow,
The Center of Ethnology and Anthropology,
Hunan Normal University,
Changsha City, Hunan Province, Peoples Republic of China

Researcher,
The World Sinology Center,
Beijing Language and Culture University,
Beijing, Peoples Republic of China

Section 1

Introduction

Chapter 1

Introductory Chapter: Corporate Governance – A Modern Perspective

Tahir Mumtaz Awan and Zohaib Riaz Pitafi

1. Introduction to corporate governance

In the early 2000s, the business world witnessed a seismic shift in the realm of corporate governance, epitomized by the fall of the Enron Corporation. Once a titan in the energy sector, Enron's collapse sent shockwaves across global markets, unveiling a startling tale of fraudulent accounting practices and corporate malfeasance. This scandal, marked by its dramatic unraveling, showcased the catastrophic consequences of poor corporate governance. Enron's deceptive financial reporting, facilitated by a complicit board of directors and a lack of transparency, not only led to its own downfall but also eroded public trust in corporate institutions at large. The Enron debacle has become a textbook example highlighting the necessity of robust and ethical governance in the corporate world. The evolution of corporate governance has been marked by significant milestones. Initially, the concept focused primarily on financial accountability, especially towards shareholders [1]. This paradigm originated in the early 20th century when businesses were often family-owned, with owners and managers being the same individuals. However, as corporations expanded and ownership became more dispersed, a gap emerged between owners and managers, necessitating more structured governance mechanisms.

Global trends have also significantly influenced corporate governance practices, necessitating adaptability and foresight from businesses worldwide. The increasing emphasis on corporate social responsibility (CSR) and sustainability has led companies to integrate environmental, social, and governance (ESG) criteria into their business strategies. Additionally, technological advancements are reshaping corporate governance. Technologies like blockchain and artificial intelligence (AI) are not only transforming business operations but also how companies are governed [2, 3]. Blockchain technology, for instance, offers unprecedented transparency and security in transactions, which can significantly enhance trust in shareholder voting processes and financial reporting. Moreover, the global business environment has become increasingly interconnected, necessitating a global perspective in governance practices. This globalization has led to the harmonization of corporate governance standards across borders, as evidenced by the widespread adoption of the OECD Principles of Corporate Governance by many countries. Such harmonization ensures that multinational corporations maintain consistent governance standards in different jurisdictions, fostering global trust and cooperation [4, 5].

Corporate governance is a fundamental framework that regulates how companies are directed and controlled. It encompasses a set of principles, practices, and processes designed to ensure that a company operates efficiently, ethically, and in the best interests of its stakeholders, including shareholders, employees, customers, and the wider community.

2. Defining the concept of corporate governance

At its core, corporate governance is about achieving a balance between the interests of a company's various stakeholders, particularly its shareholders and management. It aims to prevent conflicts of interest and promote transparency, accountability, and responsible decision-making within the organization. One crucial aspect of corporate governance is the relationship between a company's board of directors and its management team. The board of directors, elected by shareholders, is responsible for overseeing the company's strategic direction, while the management team is responsible for implementing that strategy on a day-to-day basis [5]. This separation of ownership (shareholders) and control (management) is a defining characteristic of modern corporations.

3. Elements and principles of corporate governance

To understand corporate governance fully, it is essential to explore its key elements and principles:

Shareholder Rights and Equitable Treatment: Shareholders are the owners of the company, and their rights must be respected. This includes the right to vote, receive dividends, and access relevant information. Equitable treatment ensures that all shareholders are treated fairly, regardless of their size or influence.

Board of Directors: The board plays a pivotal role in corporate governance. It is responsible for setting the company's strategic direction, appointing and overseeing the management team, and ensuring that the company operates ethically and responsibly.

Transparency and Disclosure: Companies must provide timely and accurate information about their financial performance, operations, and risks to shareholders and the public. Transparency builds trust and confidence among stakeholders.

Accountability and Responsibility: Management is accountable to the board, which, in turn, is accountable to shareholders. Corporate leaders must act in the best interests of the company and its stakeholders, making responsible decisions that align with the company's long-term objectives.

Ethical Behavior and Corporate Citizenship: Companies should operate ethically, complying with laws and regulations while also considering broader social and environmental responsibilities.

Risk Management: Effective risk management is crucial for corporate governance. Companies must identify, assess, and manage risks to ensure their long-term sustainability.

Stakeholder Engagement: Beyond shareholders, companies should consider the interests of other stakeholders, such as employees, customers, suppliers, and the communities in which they operate.

4. The modern business landscape

In the tapestry of today's society, corporations stand as central figures, deeply intertwined with the economy, communities, and a broad range of stakeholders. Their impact stretches far beyond simple financial metrics, influencing social norms, environmental sustainability, and technological advancements. As businesses navigate through an ever-changing landscape, corporate governance has become a cornerstone in ensuring ethical, sustainable, and efficient operations. The evolution of corporate governance mirrors the shifts in the business environment [6]. Traditionally, governance focused primarily on shareholder interests. However, in recent years, this view has expanded to include a wider range of stakeholders, including employees, customers, and the community at large. This change is partly a response to the growing awareness of corporate social responsibility and the realization that long-term success is tied to more than just financial performance.

Globalization and technological advancements have further reshaped the business world. The rise of digital technologies, for instance, has created new opportunities and challenges, requiring corporations to adapt their governance structures. Companies like Apple and Amazon, which have effectively harnessed technology and globalization, serve as prime examples of how dynamic governance can facilitate unprecedented growth and market dominance. Regulatory changes also play a crucial role [1, 7]. Post-2008 financial crisis reforms, such as the Dodd-Frank Act in the United States, have brought about more stringent rules, compelling companies to enhance transparency and accountability. Such regulatory environments underscore the necessity for robust governance practices, enabling organizations to not only comply with legal requirements but also to gain the trust of stakeholders and the public. Effective governance is pivotal in guiding organizations through challenges and uncertainties. Good governance practices, such as clear decision-making processes, accountability, and transparency, are crucial for managing risks and maintaining corporate integrity. As businesses confront complex issues like climate change, social inequality, and ethical conduct, strong governance frameworks can provide the strategic direction and ethical compass necessary for sustainable growth.

5. Why corporate governance matters

Implementing effective corporate governance holds immense advantages, key among them being enhanced financial performance. Good governance structures enable better decision making and risk management, factors that directly contribute to a company's financial health. This robust performance fosters investor confidence and strengthens stakeholder trust, both of which are essential for sustained success in a competitive business environment. For instance, Johnson & Johnson's enduring market presence and financial stability can be attributed in part to its strong governance principles, which have fostered a reputation for reliability and ethical conduct. Additionally, good corporate governance promotes transparency and accountability, which are vital in today's market, where information is readily available and public scrutiny is high [8]. Companies like Google and Salesforce have thrived in part due to their transparent business practices and accountable leadership. This transparency not only builds trust with stakeholders but also ensures that potential issues are identified and addressed promptly, thereby averting crises.

Another significant advantage of effective governance is the ability to attract and retain top talent. A company known for its ethical practices and good governance is more likely to attract employees who value integrity and accountability. This, in turn, fosters a positive corporate culture that contributes to employee satisfaction and retention. For example, Adobe has been recognized for its corporate culture, which is deeply rooted in strong governance and ethical practices, contributing to its high employee retention rates and consistent innovation. On the other hand, poor corporate governance can lead to severe negative outcomes, as evidenced by numerous corporate scandals. The downfall of Enron, one of the most infamous corporate collapses, stemmed largely from governance failures such as fraudulent accounting practices and lack of oversight. This not only led to the company's financial ruin but also caused significant harm to its employees, shareholders, and the wider economy [9].

More recently, Wells Fargo faced a crisis following revelations of fraudulent customer account practices, highlighting the consequences of poor internal controls and unethical behavior. Such governance failures damage the company's reputation, erode public trust, and can lead to significant legal and financial penalties. Moreover, these incidents often result in a loss of consumer and investor confidence, which can have long-lasting effects on the company's market position and financial stability. The importance of corporate governance in today's business landscape cannot be overstated. Effective governance practices lead to improved financial performance, increased transparency and accountability, and a stronger corporate reputation, all of which are crucial for long-term success. Conversely, neglecting governance can result in significant financial, legal, and reputational damage. As the corporate world continues to evolve, the need for robust and adaptable governance frameworks becomes increasingly critical [10].

Thus, as corporations navigate an increasingly complex and dynamic business environment, the role of corporate governance becomes ever more critical. The challenges of cybersecurity, sustainability, and diversity demand innovative and adaptive governance approaches. Good corporate governance is no longer a luxury but a necessity, pivotal for ensuring long-term success and sustainability in today's global economy.

6. Challenges and evolutions

Corporate governance, in its contemporary form, navigates a landscape rife with multifaceted challenges, each demanding innovative and nuanced responses. Among these challenges, cybersecurity stands out as a critical concern in the digital era. High-profile incidents, such as the Facebook data breach, have shed light on the severe vulnerabilities and consequences that lapses in governance can precipitate. These breaches not only lead to immediate financial losses but also long-term damage to reputation and stakeholder trust. In response, there is a growing emphasis on incorporating robust cybersecurity measures into governance frameworks, making it an integral part of risk management strategies. Furthermore, sustainability has ascended to the forefront of corporate governance concerns. Environmental and social consciousness is no longer peripheral but central to corporate strategy [11]. Companies like Unilever and Patagonia are trailblazers in this regard, embedding sustainability into their core business philosophies. This shift is not just about corporate image but is also driven by the recognition that long-term business success is inextricably linked to environmental stewardship and social responsibility. These companies demonstrate how sustainable practices can be aligned with profitability, challenging the traditional view that environmental and social goals are secondary to financial objectives [12].

The emphasis on diversity and inclusion reflects another significant evolution in corporate governance. A diverse array of perspectives in leadership and workforce is increasingly seen as a key driver of innovation and resilience. The push for diversity is not just about gender but also encompasses race, ethnicity, age, and different life experiences. Initiatives like the Women on Boards movement, aiming to increase female representation in boardrooms, have gained considerable momentum. These initiatives are supported by a growing body of research suggesting that diverse boards and leadership teams can lead to better decision-making and financial performance [5, 13]. The approach to corporate governance also varies widely across different regions, influenced by cultural, legal, and economic factors. In countries like Japan and South Korea, governance structures are often marked by a focus on consensus and long-term relationships, reflecting deeper cultural inclinations toward collectivism. This stands in contrast to the more individualistic and shareholder-focused approaches prevalent in the United States and Europe. These regional differences highlight the need for a flexible and context-specific approach to corporate governance.

Global standards and initiatives, such as the OECD Principles of Corporate Governance, play a crucial role in shaping these varied practices. They offer a blueprint for effective governance that balances the interests of various stakeholders while promoting transparency and accountability. These principles are not just theoretical constructs but have been instrumental in guiding reforms and shaping governance practices worldwide. They demonstrate the growing recognition of the need for a cohesive global approach to governance, one that can adapt to the unique challenges and dynamics of the modern business world. The current state of corporate governance is one of dynamic evolution, responding to the challenges posed by digitalization, environmental concerns, and the increasing importance of diversity and inclusion. As governance practices continue to evolve, they must remain agile and responsive, capable of addressing the unique demands of an ever-changing global business environment [13].

Additionally, good corporate governance promotes transparency and accountability, which are vital in today's market, where information is readily available and public scrutiny is high [11]. This not only led to the company's financial ruin but also caused significant harm to its employees, shareholders, and the wider economy [12].

As the corporate world continues to evolve, the need for robust and adaptable governance frameworks becomes increasingly critical [13].

Acknowledgements

The author acknowledges the use of an AI tool for language polishing of the manuscript.

Author details

Tahir Mumtaz Awan[1,2*] and Zohaib Riaz Pitafi[1]

1 Department of Management Sciences, COMSATS University Islamabad, Pakistan

2 School of Business Sciences, University of the Witwatersrand, Johannesburg, South Africa

*Address all correspondence to: tahir_mumtaz@comsats.edu.pk

References

[1] Monks RA, Minow N. Corporate Governance. USA: John Wiley & Sons; 2011

[2] Kavadis N, Thomsen S. Sustainable corporate governance: A review of research on long-term corporate ownership and sustainability. Corporate Governance: An International Review. 2023;**31**(1):198-226

[3] Brennan NM, Subramaniam N, Van Staden CJ. Corporate Governance Implications of Disruptive Technology: An Overview. United Kingdom: Elsevier; 2019. p. 100860

[4] Fenwick M, Vermeulen EP. Technology and corporate governance: Blockchain, crypto, and artificial intelligence. The Texas Journal of Business Law. 2019;**48**:1

[5] Cheffins BR. The History of Corporate Governance. United Kingdom: Oxford University Press, UK; 2013

[6] Grant GH. The evolution of corporate governance and its impact on modern corporate America. Management Decision. 2003;**41**(9):923-934

[7] Khan H. A literature review of corporate governance. In: International Conference on E-business, Management and Economics. Singapore: IACSIT Press; 2011

[8] Báez AB et al. Gender diversity, corporate governance and firm behavior: The challenge of emotional management. European Research on Management and Business Economics. 2018;**24**(3):121-129

[9] Solomon J. Corporate Governance and Accountability. United Kingdom: John Wiley & Sons; 2020

[10] Vanishvili M, Shanava Z. Challenges and perspectives of corporate governance in Georgia. American Research Journal of Humanities & Social Science (ARJHSS) R. 2022;**5**(04):118-127

[11] Williamson OE. On the governance of the modern corporation. Hofstra Law Review. 1979;**8**:63

[12] Mees B. Corporate governance as a reform movement. Journal of Management History. 2015;**21**(2):194-209

[13] Ha TTH. Modern corporate governance standards and role of auditing-cases in some Western european countries after financial crisis, corporate scandals and manipulation. International Journal of Entrepreneurship. 2019;**23**:1-15

Section 2

Corporate Governance: A New Era

Chapter 2

Integration of ESG Criteria in Financial Education

Carmen Pénnanen-Arias, Nicolás Barrientos-Oradini, David Álvarez-Maldonado, Carlos Aparicio Puentes and Víctor Manuel Yáñez Jara

Abstract

The article highlights the absence of ESG criteria in financial education, risking economic, and ethical implications by neglecting future well-being. The bibliometric situation regarding financial education and ESG is assessed. Within this framework, the need to incorporate ESG factors in profitability evaluation is emphasized, particularly in adjusting discount rates to account for their impact. Moreover, it is possible to incorporate available data from Refinitiv to work with empirical material in academic processes. Including ESG variables in cash flow evaluation is crucial for comprehensive assessment. The article concludes by advocating for corporate governance standards that reflect the long-term sustainability impacts and the full integration of ESG factors into financial education.

Keywords: general economics, ESG, teaching, education, social responsibility

1. Introduction

International financial education generally overlooks the integration of environmental, social, and governance (ESG) criteria [1–11]. These criteria are not incorporated into most profitability evaluations of various economic activities unless national legislation mandates their inclusion [9, 12]. This can be evidenced by the scant scientific production on the subject.

To provide a more detailed examination of specific case studies demonstrating ESG integration, an analysis was conducted on the Web of Science (WOS) platform. Using the Boolean search formula ALL = (Financial Education AND ESG), the result yields an insufficient 227 results, indicating a small number of scientific articles. This scientific productivity is described below using bibliometric indicators.

Table 1 shows that document-level productivity is highest in China, with 68 documents to date. China also leads the citation index with 617 citations, followed by countries like Canada and England at a considerable distance. Additionally, **Figure 1** illustrates that China leads in citations and collaborative works in terms of co-authorship, establishing itself as the most significant cluster.

Country	Documents	Citations
China	68	617
Canada	23	209
England	22	408
Italy	20	327
Malaysia	19	304
Spain	16	140
Russia	15	86
Japan	14	572
USA	13	166
Australia	10	316
Brazil	9	58
France	8	165

Source: Own elaboration based on Web of Science.

Table 1.
Scientific productivity in financial education and ESG.

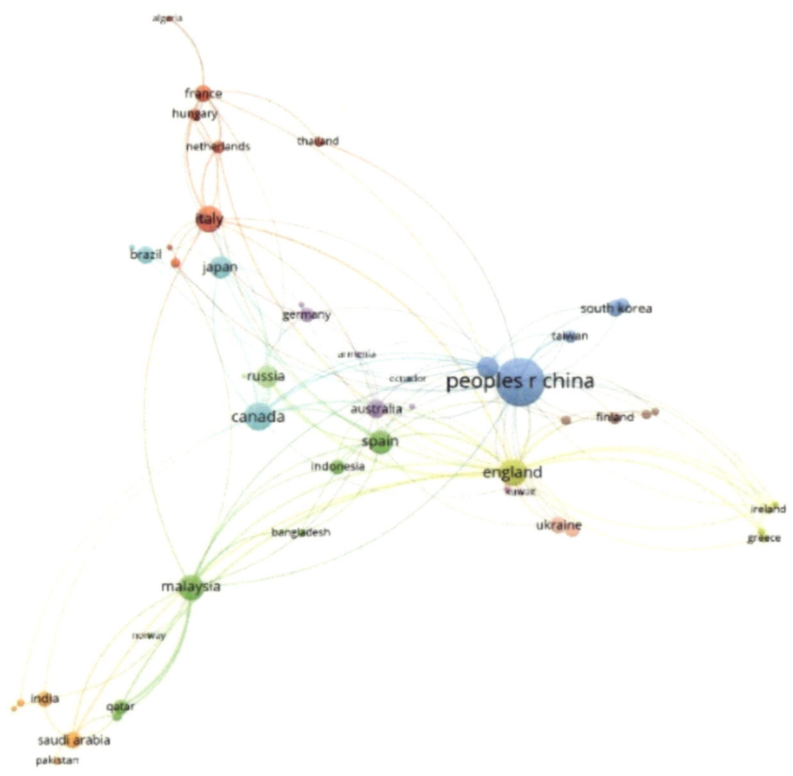

Figure 1.
Scientific productivity by country and co-authorship between countries. Source: Own elaboration using VOSviewer.

Authors	Documents	Citations
Managi, S.	2	398
Fujii, H.	1	357
Nozawa, W.	1	357
Xie, J.	1	357
Yagi, M.	1	357
Choo, Esg.	4	229
Xue, J.	4	229
Tang, X.	2	162
Kang, J.	2	151
Guo, Y.	1	151
Li, D.	1	151
Wu, M.	1	151

Source: Own elaboration based on Web of Science.

Table 2.
Author influence based on citations.

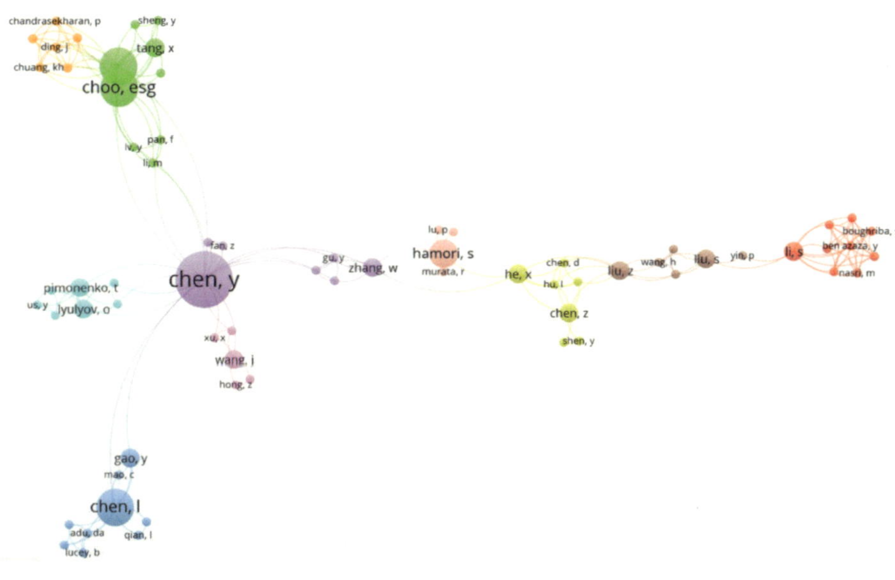

Figure 2.
Co-authorship based on citation influence. Source: Own elaboration using VOSviewer.

Table 2 highlights the most influential authors based on citation indicators, showing that Managi leads the list with 398 citations, followed by Fujii with 357, Nozawa with 357, Xie with 357, Yagi with 357, and Choo with 229, among other authors. This can also be represented in terms of co-authorships in **Figure 2**.

Table 3 shows the most relevant institutions in scientific productivity regarding Financial Education and ESG. The University of Quebec Montreal leads with six

Institutions	Documents	Citations
Univ. Quebec Montreal	6	55
Sapienza Univ. Rome	5	179
Univ. Teknol Malaysia	5	96
CEPR	5	58
Peter Great St. Petersburg Polytech Univ.	5	19
Kobe Univ.	4	413
Natl Univ. Singapore.	4	229
Capital Univ. Econ & Business.	4	76
Minist Educ & Higher Educ.	4	69
Univ. Teknol Mara.	4	45
Hong Kong Polytech Univ.	4	19
King Faisal Univ.	4	11

Source: Own elaboration based on Web of Science.

Table 3.
Documentary scientific productivity of institutions.

documents, followed by Sapienza University of Rome with five documents, Universiti Teknologi Malaysia with five documents, CEPR with five documents, and Peter the Great St. Petersburg Polytechnic University with five documents. This is also reflected in institutional co-authorship in **Figure 3**, led by the University of Quebec Montreal.

This lack of scientific productivity could be related to the difficulty in accessing relevant, valid, and reliable ESG data from organizations. This problem could be resolved by using the Refinitiv platform to access ESG data and integrate it into financial education and scientific research. The Refinitiv ESG data application is a powerful and versatile tool, ideal for those looking to integrate sustainable and responsible practices into financial education and scientific research.

With access to detailed information on the ESG performance of over 14,000 publicly listed companies, the application covers approximately 80% of global market capitalization, providing a solid data foundation for analysis and informed decision-making. To access this data, a search must be performed in Workspace by entering the company's name or code followed by a space and the word "ESG," generating a Sustainability Data Panel. The Sustainability Panel is a window into the extensive range of sustainability data offered by LSEG. Here, students and scientists can explore customizable thematic cards covering topics from sustainable finance to greenhouse gas emissions. Each card can be exported and used in academic presentations or research reports, facilitating comparative analysis between different companies and sectors.

Additionally, the ESG Statement tab is essential for those seeking a deep understanding of a company's ESG performance. Here, both reported and standardized data are presented, along with detailed scores at the metric, category, pillar, and summary levels. The audit functions allow access to source documents, which is invaluable for validating data and ensuring transparency in scientific research. The ESG data sheet is a flexible tool for creating personalized reports. Educators can use this section to teach students how to select comparable peers, define relevant ESG topics, and add critical commentary. Generated reports can be saved

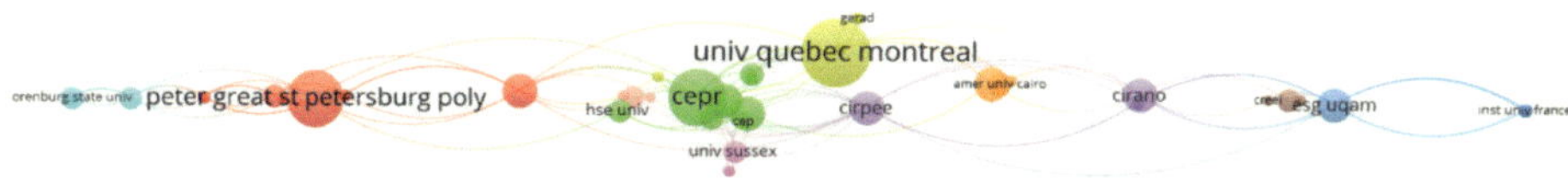

Figure 3.
Co-authorship of the documentary scientific productivity of institutions. Source: Own elaboration using VOSviewer.

and published, providing a practical resource for class projects and academic publications.

For a comprehensive view of a company's ESG score components, the ESG Score Profile tab is fundamental. It allows for the identification of specific strengths and weaknesses and breaks down the scores into pillars, categories, and individual metrics. This visualization capability is particularly useful in scientific research to determine areas for improvement and analyze trends in sustainable practices. In this context, the ESG Peer Analysis tab facilitates comparison between a company and its competitors. Using this tool in financial education allows students to apply customized filters, add additional data, and use pre-existing templates or create new ones for comparative analysis. This is essential for understanding how companies position themselves within their industry in terms of sustainability.

The Sustainable Finance Disclosure Regulation (SFDR) tab provides ESG disclosure standards, detailing the closest peers by market capitalization. This section is crucial for assessing a company's performance and accessing original data, offering a solid basis for academic research and teaching sustainable financial regulations. The FTSE Russell Green Revenues tab shows companies' performance concerning ESG scores, used for investment decisions and dialog with portfolio companies. The scores also determine the constituents of the FTSE Blossom Japan and FTSE4Good indexes, information that can be used in case studies in financial education.

The EU Taxonomy tab helps understand the alignment of business activities with European regulations for sustainable activities. Students can analyze how a company's revenues are distributed by segments and its compliance with environmental objectives, providing a practical approach to teaching environmental regulations and their impact on business operations. ESG scores are relative indicators that evaluate a company's performance at multiple levels. Refinitiv Datastream offers access to over 600 ESG measures, facilitating detailed analysis. The Diversity and Inclusion (D&I) scores measure workplace diversity and inclusion performance, based on pillars like diversity, inclusion, people development, and controversies. This information is vital for research aimed at promoting equitable and diverse work environments.

ESG bonds are debt instruments aimed at specific environmental, social, or governance purposes. Types include equality bonds, impact bonds, pandemic bonds, social bonds, sustainability bonds, vaccine bonds, project bonds, and transition bonds, offering a wide range of options for financing sustainable projects. These bonds are a central topic in modern financial education, providing practical examples of how investments can align with ESG objectives.

Thus, the Refinitiv ESG application is an essential tool for both financial education and scientific research. It offers a wide range of data and analyses that allow users to make informed decisions, promote sustainable practices, and contribute to the development of a more responsible and transparent financial market.

On the Refinitiv platform, various calculations can be performed with ESG data. To illustrate the methods used to evaluate the impact of ESG factors on profitability, the following calculations could be performed by downloading ESG data from Refinitiv, which offers one of the most comprehensive databases, covering more than 80% of global market capitalization, with over 700 different ESG metrics and a significant historical record. Data can be downloaded in various formats such as CSV, JSON, PDF, Python, SQL, Text, and XML.

The types of calculations that can be performed with ESG data include:

a. ESG scores: Refinitiv offers ESG scores that transparently and objectively measure a company's performance, engagement, and effectiveness in ESG across 10 main themes. These scores are designed to integrate and represent industry relevance and company size biases. You can use these scores to compare the ESG performance of different companies.

b. Trend analysis: You can analyze the trends over time of a company's or a group of companies' ESG scores, identifying which companies are improving their ESG performance.

c. Comparison between companies: You can compare the ESG scores of different companies within the same industry to identify leaders and laggards.

d. Correlation analysis: You can analyze the correlation between ESG scores and other financial indicators to see if there is any relationship.

e. Regression analysis: You can use ESG scores as independent variables in a regression model to investigate their impact on different dependent variables, such as stock performance or stock price volatility.

f. Time series analysis: With Refinitiv ESG data going back to 2002, you can perform time series analysis to examine how companies' ESG scores have evolved over time and how these trends correlate with other financial indicators.

g. Panel analysis: With ESG data covering more than 88% of global market capitalization, you can perform panel analysis to investigate the fixed and random effects of ESG scores on companies.

h. Prediction models: You can use ESG scores as predictors in machine learning models to predict future financial performance, risks, etc.

The Refinitiv platform and its ESG data enable the development of practical steps and strategies for educators and institutions to integrate ESG factors into their curricula. In this context of financial education [5, 10, 13], there is often an emphasis on applying widely accepted general formulas found in specialized literature. These formulas are applicable to different economic realities worldwide [2, 3, 8, 14–16]. However, it is evident that communities and social environments increasingly demand the inclusion of environmental and social considerations in the evaluation of economic activities [4, 12, 17]. Additionally, a governance approach is required to compel the consideration of these impacts [1, 8, 12, 16, 18–22]. Externalities, indirect effects not reflected through price mechanisms, are defined by economic theory as factors causing private prices to differ from social prices [3, 6, 16, 23, 24]. The lack of legislation mandating the valuation of these indirect effects in environmental and social terms leads to the omission of these collateral effects when evaluating the private profitability of an investment [12]. Consequently, negative aspects may be considered as social costs, often justified by the positive benefits of economic activity, such as job creation and higher incomes [1–11, 20]. However, this classification as profitable and the promotion of these activities as socially contributory may lack solid foundations [8, 13]. **Figure 4** below represents the negative externality represented by these social costs:

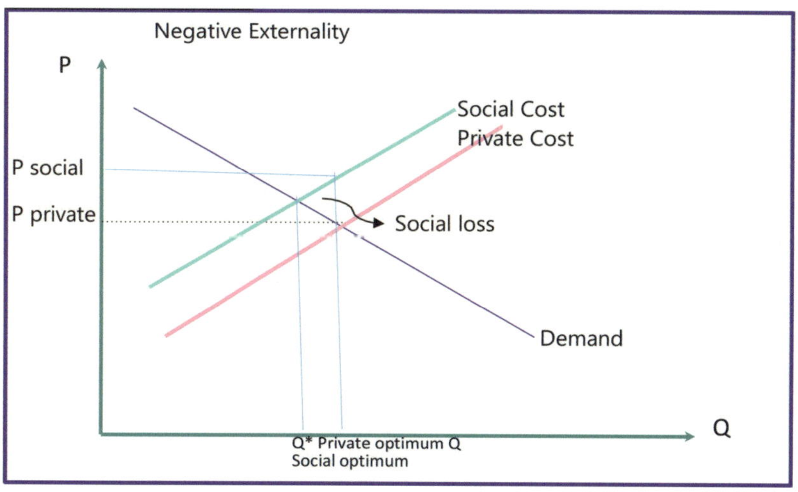

Figure 4.
Negative externality. Source: Own elaboration.

In this context, the question arises as to whether omitting the consideration of environmental, social, and governance (ESG) variables constitutes an adequate strategy [3, 6, 9, 16, 23, 25]. From a reductionist and short-term oriented perspective, it might be perceived as such; however, from the viewpoint of a society whose primary imperative is its long-term survival and therefore the guarantee of its sustainability, evaluating economic activities based on their contribution to sustainability becomes a crucial aspect [16, 26–30]. This article addresses the exclusion of ESG variables in the evaluation and execution of economic activities, which raises the possibility that current generations may give greater weight to their own well-being than that of future generations [9, 16, 21, 22]. This phenomenon constitutes a matter of ethical relevance, in the understanding that ethics, from the perspective of sustainability, implies justice in terms of intergenerational equity in access to essential goods and services for life on the planet [31–34]. Consequently, the omission of considering ESG variables not only poses challenges from an economic standpoint but also presents substantial ethical implications regarding equity and responsibility toward future generations [1–11, 16, 21, 22, 28, 30, 35].

2. Environmental context

Currently, significant impacts of climate change affecting our planet are evident, manifesting, for example, through unprecedented floods [8, 16, 22]. These destructive events ravage everything in their path, affecting homes, agriculture, and causing considerable environmental damage. The recovery from such effects entails substantial costs for those affected. Additionally, large-scale wildfires have been witnessed, not only in inhabited areas but also in forest reserves and agricultural areas, with significant economic consequences, including impoverishment and displacement of affected local populations [8, 16, 21, 22].

Moreover, every year we experience extremely cold temperatures in winter, requiring considerable investments in heating, and unusually high temperatures in summer, demanding investments in air conditioning. These circumstances lead to the conclusion that activities that have contributed to environmental damage and climate change have been underestimated in terms of their real profitability. This is due to the omission in the evaluation of these negative impacts [1–3, 5–8, 10, 16].

Given this landscape, it is evident that the incorporation of environmental, social, and governance considerations is imperative before authorizing the execution of productive initiatives [4, 12, 13]. Therefore, integrating concepts of financial sustainability into the academic curricula of future professionals in this field becomes an urgent need [26, 35]. This will ensure that future professionals have a comprehensive understanding of relevant variables in the process of calculating the true profitability of an investment [17]. It will also enable them to distinguish truly contributory activities in the long term from those that are only profitable under a short-sighted and limited evaluation framework, without considering sustainability, understood as a long-term survival imperative [8, 16, 21, 22].

3. Sustainable discount rate

The discount rate, used to discount the net cash flows derived from economic activities and assess their contribution to wealth generation, reflects the opportunity cost of funds used in financing such activities. However, by not incorporating environmental, social, and governance (ESG) factors into its calculation, there is a possibility of underestimating the required profitability [12, 17]. This risk is magnified when a project, although seemingly profitable under conventional analysis, generates unconsidered environmental damages or negative social effects not accounted for by governance standards regulating such activity, resulting in net negative impacts on the real and long-term financial sustainability of the project [8, 16, 21, 22, 26].

It is important to note that when calculating discount rates for a specific economic activity, risk coefficients, betas, derived from similar activities carried out in foreign countries, particularly in the United States, are often used. However, risk factors are not necessarily equivalent, as environmental regulations and governance requirements often differ significantly between developed and emerging countries. While betas from developed countries may more accurately reflect certain negative impacts, such as generic environmental ones, they do not guarantee a proper assessment of specific social impacts and other environmental factors related to indigenous flora and fauna in emerging economies. Thus, the use of external betas can distort the calculation of the true opportunity cost or sustainable discount rate in a specific national context [1, 8, 16]. Similarly, the use of betas based on internal data from the home economy, with more lenient sustainability regulations, can also lead to distortions by not properly evaluating the true risk associated with an activity. This practice carries the danger of underestimating such risk, resulting in the overvaluation of the real profitability of a specific project.

Furthermore, the traditional formula for calculating the discount rate incorporates the excess return earned by the market. Since this return does not stem from activities considering ESG factors in their evaluation, there is an additional risk of generating a second distortion. Consequently, it is evident that a discount rate calculated conventionally may underestimate the true required profitability of an activity, especially when carried out in different socio-environmental and governance contexts [8].

$$\underbrace{\overline{R_i}}_{\text{Expected Return of the Asset}} = \underbrace{R_F}_{\text{Risk- Free Rate}} + \underbrace{\beta_i}_{\text{Asset Beta}} \times \underbrace{(\overline{R_M} - R_F)}_{\text{Market Risk Premium}} \quad (1)$$

Eq. (1) illustrates how incorporating sustainability risks into betas, as well as including environmental, social, and governance (ESG) variables in the calculation of the real return of the average market, affects the required return on assets. It is evident that the less consideration given to social and environmental impact, due to more lenient corporate governance regulations, the greater the discrepancy between the required return and the true opportunity cost of the resources employed in that activity.

4. The impact of financing structure on sustainability

In the previous section, the topic of discount rates was addressed, focusing on the risk associated with the exclusion of relevant variables linked to the true risk of investment.

This risk is not fully reflected in the risk coefficients inherent to the activity and the market, as impacts not internalized by legal standards in the environment are omitted. However, it is also crucial to mention the impact of the financing structure, as debt is commonly attributed with the benefit of reducing the opportunity cost of capital [8, 36].

Nevertheless, it is important to highlight valuable contributions in the literature of sustainable corporate finance that evidence the negative impact that financing through debt can have on long-term sustainability [37]. This is due, among other reasons, to the fact that the owners of such capital often are unaware of the true environmental and social impact they might be contributing to finance, in exchange for the perception of an interest payment [8, 16, 22].

In this sense, financial leverage, while it may seemingly reduce the cost of capital, could generate negative externalities not considered by investors and lenders. The lack of complete information about the environmental and social risks associated with debt-financed projects can lead to an inadequate assessment of the true opportunity cost and, therefore, affect the long-term sustainability of investments [2, 3, 8].

This approach highlights the importance of considering not only the inherent risks of the investment itself but also the risks associated with the financing structure used. Sustainable financial management must take into account not only short-term financial profitability but also long-term impacts in terms of economic, environmental, and social sustainability [8, 35].

$$\text{WACC} = ks\,(\text{S/V}) + kd\,(1 - \zeta c)(\text{B/V}) \quad (2)$$

where: WACC = weighted average cost of capital; kd = after-tax cost of debt; ks = cost of equity; ζc = corporate tax rate; S = equity; B = debt; V = S + B = enterprise value.

Eq. (2) reveals that the cost of capital, being a weighted average between the return required by equity owners and the return demanded by creditors, could be underestimated if environmental, social, and governance (ESG) considerations are omitted from its calculation. The inclusion of these considerations could result in an increase in the required return both from shareholders, due to a heightened perception of risk, and from creditors, by integrating into their analysis the valuation requirements of the real impact of the investments they are financing [3, 8].

In this context, the omission of ESG variables in the calculation of the cost of capital could lead to an incomplete assessment of the risks associated with an investment. Shareholders, by not considering relevant environmental and social factors, could underestimate the risk and demand a lower return than necessary. On the other hand, creditors may not be adequately considering the risks associated with the activities they finance, which could affect risk perception and increase the required return.

In summary, the incorporation of ESG considerations in the calculation of the cost of capital is essential to accurately reflect the real risk and impacts associated with an investment. This inclusion would not only be consistent with sustainable financial practices but also help ensure a more accurate assessment of costs and benefits over time [12, 13, 27].

5. Cash flows and sustainability

Considering that environmental, social, and governance (ESG) factors can affect the required profitability of different investments, it is crucial to highlight that cash flows are also impacted by the inclusion or exclusion of these factors in their quantification.

Historically, we have witnessed the formation of significant fortunes based on the overexploitation of non-renewable natural resources, environmental damage, and social and labor dumping practices, among others [38, 39]. These practices, which were not anticipated or sanctioned at the time, demonstrate a failure in the legal and corporate governance norms that were in place during the occurrence of these investments [37]. The consequence of these omissions is the attainment of cash flows greater than those that would have been generated if the social and environmental costs of productive activities had been properly internalized [9, 12, 17]. This results in the generation of additional wealth based on the transfer of long-term welfare and future generations' well-being to the generations of that time, as well as from disadvantaged social groups to the beneficiaries.

In this context, it is imperative to consider the effect of ESG variables when determining the residual cash flows generated by an economic activity. This implies that residual cash flows must incorporate both total costs and benefits, not just those directly perceived by the investor or project owner [17]. The inclusion of ESG factors in the quantification of cash flows ensures a more holistic and accurate assessment of the social and environmental impacts associated with an investment, thus enabling a more informed and ethical decision-making process. Furthermore, this consideration helps to avoid the attainment of benefits at the expense of negative externalities transferred to society and the environment.

6. Discussion

The true sustainability of a company is manifested when its net present value is positive, considering the incorporation of all environmental and social effects in the total calculation of long-term cash flows, discounted at a rate of return that reflects the effects of the financing structure and the total risk, both private and social, associated with that activity [40–42].

In other words, it is proposed that the intertemporal viability for society, considering job creation, services, and products, must be positive for a particular economic activity to be genuinely sustainable. This implies that legal standards play a fundamental role in contributing to making this approach effective, by generating the appropriate incentives for private agents [17, 29]. The replacement of private initiative is not proposed, but rather the implementation of correct incentives through legal regulations and corporate governance [37]. The goal is to align short-term private interests with the long-term survival interest of society.

It is essential to highlight that, in the absence of appropriate incentives, individual optimization tends to prevail, where each actor seeks to maximize their particular profitability within the rules that govern them [9]. However, it is evident that the optimization of parts leads to the suboptimization of the whole. In this context, the general welfare and long-term sustainability of society are threatened by short-sighted practices and permissive standards that do not impose the consideration of the indirect effects of economic activities on other agents, other activities, or future generations. The need for adequate incentives and standards that promote the comprehensive consideration of social and environmental impacts is fundamental to ensuring genuine sustainability in economic decision-making [41, 42].

The omission of environmental, social, and governance (ESG) considerations in evaluating the real contribution of various economic activities to financial sustainability underscores the fundamental importance of defining corporate governance standards that regulate such activities [29, 37].

If the standards do not reflect medium and long-term impacts and do not require their inclusion, speaking of financial sustainability becomes a concept more desirable than feasible [17]. However, the high cost that the omission of environmental and social impact is having on communities makes a paradigm shift imperative, moving from simple growth to truly sustainable growth.

The evolution of finance education has followed a different direction, where the application of increasingly sophisticated mathematical and statistical models tends to obscure or overlook a deeper assessment of what is becoming increasingly evident. Education must incorporate concepts of social and environmental cost and benefit, intrinsically linked to intergenerational ethics. Concepts of circular economy, reuse, and recycling must be integrated, all fundamental to financial sustainability, which should be the primary goal to maintain the long-term viability of communities [26, 35, 37].

Real-world problems require tangible solutions. When not all aspects associated with the impact of economic activity are addressed, we encounter highly sophisticated explanatory models that, however, cannot predict anything due to the omission of relevant variables present in the real world and that have not been incorporated into the analysis because there is no explicit obligation to consider them [29]. The dilemma lies in continuing with intellectual and blackboard exercises or addressing real problems that must be urgently addressed. Financial education and practice must evolve to reflect the complexity and interconnectedness of the factors influencing true financial sustainability [26].

7. Conclusions

The article highlights the omission of ESG factors in current financial education and evidences the activity and scientific productivity in this field through a bibliometric analysis in Web of Science. Additionally, it examines methods for utilizing ESG factors using data provided by the Refinitiv platform, suggesting statistical and econometric analyses to support financial analyses with ESG criteria.

Thus, it is observed how ESG data is reported and utilized on the Refinitiv platform, with the development of an introductory guide for its use and integration into financial education. This guide proposes incorporating ESG factors into educational curricula and developing new lines of research using this integrated database.

Up to this point, we have examined the proper evaluation of the profitability of an economic activity and the factors that should be considered in this process, breaking down the relevant components. However, the purpose of this document is to provide a basic framework to serve as a guide when evaluating the impact of an economic activity on sustainability [37].

It is crucial to highlight that each activity has its own characteristics, and the contribution of this document lies in clarifying which components or variables of the evaluation process should receive special attention and incorporating environmental, social, and governance (ESG) criteria in the assessment.

The evolution of communications and the globalization of the economy have contributed to raising awareness in society about the impact of ignoring the effects not internalized in the production process. There is a growing social consensus that sustainability is paramount, and therefore, it is essential to consider the various rights involved in carrying out economic activities [26]. In simple terms, it is becoming increasingly evident that omitting the consideration of stakeholders will no longer be a viable option in the near future [8, 11, 43–47].

Author details

Carmen Pénnanen-Arias[1], Nicolás Barrientos-Oradini[2,3], David Álvarez-Maldonado[4*], Carlos Aparicio Puentes[5] and Víctor Manuel Yáñez Jara[6]

1 Economy and Administration Committee of the CNA, Santiago, Chile

2 Faculty of Economics and Business, Alberto Hurtado University, Chile

3 School of Management and Business, Miguel de Cervantes University, Chile

4 Universidad Tecnológica Metropolitana de Chile (UTEM), Chile

5 Universidad Miguel de Cervantes, Chile

6 Universidad Andrés Bello, Chile

*Address all correspondence to: david.alvarez@utem.cl

References

[1] Andreu A. Estándares para el Reporte de Sostenibilidad: Dónde Estamos y Dónde Llegaremos. 2022. Available from: https://bit.ly/3UHpwKA

[2] Andreu A, Castilla A. Información Financiera VS Información no Financiera: Cuestión de Madurez. 2022. Available from: http://bit.ly/3USLDxg

[3] Blowfield M, Murray A. Corporate Responsibility; A Critical Introduction. USA: Oxford University Press; 2008

[4] Bruno CC, Henisz WJ. Environmental, social, and governance (ESG) outcomes and municipal credit risk. Business & Society. 2024. DOI: 10.1177/00076503231220541

[5] Cornell B, Shapiro A. Corporate stakeholders and corporate finance. Financial Management. Spring; 1987;**16**(1):5-14. DOI: 10.2307/3665543

[6] Fergus AHT, Rowney JIA. Sustainable development: Lost meaning and opportunity? Journal of Business Ethics. 2005;**60**:17-27. DOI: 10.1007/s10551-005-2927-9

[7] Hobbs A, Linn J. Will There be a 'Next' if Corporate Governance is Focused on the 'Now'? EY – Global; 2021. Available from: https://www.ey.com/en_gl/

[8] Martínez SS. Environmental accounting in the finances of sustainable companies in Mexico. Revista de Gestão Social e Ambiental. 2022;**16**(2):1-15. DOI: 10.24857/rgsa.v16n2-009

[9] Martínez-Ferrero J, Ramón-Llorens MC, García-Meca E. CEO narcissism and ESG misconduct. Research in International Business and Finance. 2024;**69**:102284. DOI: 10.1016/j.ribaf.2024.102284

[10] Orlitzky M, Benjamin JD. Corporate social performance and firm risk: A meta-analytic review. Business & Society. 2001;**40**:369-396. DOI: 10.1177/000765030104000402

[11] Zsolnai L. Ethics in the Economy. Bern: Peter Lang; 2002

[12] Aboud A, Saleh A, Eliwa Y. Does mandating ESG reporting reduce ESG decoupling? Evidence from the European Union's directive 2014/95. Business Strategy and the Environment. 2024;**33**(2):1305-1320. DOI: 10.1002/bse.3543

[13] Jun W, Shiyong Z, Yi T. Does ESG disclosure help improve intangible capital? Evidence from A-share listed companies. Frontiers in Environmental Science. 2022;**10**:858548. DOI: 10.3389/fenvs.2022.858548

[14] CDP. CDP Technical Note: Relevance of Scope 3 Categories by Sector. CDP; 2022. Available from: https://cdn.cdp.net/cdp

[15] COSO.ORG. Guidance on Enterprise Risk Management. 2022. Available from: https://www.coso.org/guidance

[16] Palacio JRS, Climent VC. Economía del Bien Común y finanzas éticas. CIRIEC-España. 2018;**93**:241-264. ISSN: 1989-6816

[17] Sheehan NT, Vaidyanathan G, Fox KA, Klassen M. Making the invisible, visible: Overcoming barriers to ESG performance with an ESG mindset. Business Horizons. 2023;**66**(2):265-276. DOI: 10.1016/j.bushor.2022.07.003

[18] Ballentine M, Callahan W, Fava SJ, Sottong J, Stanway J, Wickwire S. Corporate Value Chain (Scope 3) Accounting and

Reporting Standard. Supplement to the GHG Protocol Corporate Accounting and Reporting Standard. GHG Protocol Team; 2011. Available from: http://bit.ly/3E4dL9Y

[19] EFQM. Organisational Change Management. EFQM; 2022. Available from: https://efqm.org/

[20] Jeucken M. Sustainability in Finance—A Retroductive Exploration. Rotterdam: Erasmus University; 2004

[21] PwC, WAS. Sostenibilidad en los Consejos y en la Alta Dirección. 2020. Available from: http://bit.ly/3O4WXo1

[22] Roger C. El Sistema de Control Interno de la Información No Financiera (SCIINF). 2022. Available from: http://bit.ly/3hCsYr7

[23] Boadi K. The Concept of Sustainable Development: A Critical Analysis [Internet]. 2002. Available from: www.ises.abo.fi/kurser/nat/Ecolecon/Seminars/Kwasi_boadi_Sust_dev.pdf

[24] Brounen D, Marcato G, Op't Veld H. Pricing ESG equity ratings and underlying data in listed real estate securities. Sustainability. 2021;**13**(4):2037. DOI: 10.3390/su13042037

[25] Haigh M, Hazelton J. Financial markets: A tool for social responsibility? Journal of Business Ethics. 2004;**52**:59-71. DOI: 10.1023/B:BUSI.0000033107.22587.0b

[26] Carroll AB. The pyramid of corporate social responsibility: Toward the moral management of organizational stakeholders. Business Horizons. 1991;**34**(4):39-48. Available from: https://www.jstor.org/stable/3857969

[27] Helfaya A, Morris R, Aboud A. Investigating the factors that determine the ESG disclosure practices in Europe. Sustainability. 2023;**15**(6):5508. DOI: 10.3390/su15065508

[28] Kakabadse NK et al. Corporate social responsibility and stakeholder approach: A conceptual review. International Journal of Business Governance and Ethics. 2005;**1**:277-302. DOI: 10.1504/IJBGE.2005.006733

[29] Li Y, Gong M, Zhang XY, Koh L. The impact of environmental, social, and governance disclosure on firm value: The role of CEO power. The British Accounting Review. 2018;**50**(1):60-75. DOI: 10.1016/j.bar.2017.09.007

[30] Louche C. Ethical Investments; Processes and Mechanisms of Institutionalisation in the Netherlands, 1990-2002. Erasmus Center for Sustainable Development y Management (ESM). Rotterdam: Erasmus University; 2004. ISBN: 90-77595-48-1

[31] Bernholdt D, Bharathi S, Brown D, Chanchio K, Chen M, Chervenak A, et al. The earth system grid: Supporting the next generation of climate modeling research. Proceedings of the IEEE. 2005;**93**(3):485-495. DOI: 10.1109/JPROC.2004.842745

[32] Huang L, Chen A. Family business succession and corporate ESG behavior. Finance Research Letters. 2024;**60**:104901. DOI: 10.1016/j.frl.2023.104901

[33] Sætra HS. The AI ESG protocol: Evaluating and disclosing the environment, social, and governance implications of artificial intelligence capabilities, assets, and activities. Sustainable Development. 2023;**31**(2):1027-1037. DOI: 10.1002/sd.2438

[34] Tanguay GA, Rajaonson J, Lefebvre JF, Lanoie P. Measuring the

sustainability of cities: An analysis of the use of local indicators. Ecological Indicators. 2010;**10**(2):407-418. DOI: 10.1016/j.ecolind.2009.07.013

[35] Carroll AB, Adler NJ, Mintzberg H, Cooren F, Suddaby R, Freeman RE. What 'are' responsible management? A conceptual potluck. In: Laasch O, Suddaby R, Freeman RE, Jamali D, editors. The Research Handbook of Responsible Management. Cheltenham: Edward Elgar; 2020. ISBN: 978-1-78897-195-9

[36] Schmidheiny S. Changing Course: A Global Business Perspective on Development and the Environment. Cambridge: MIT Press; 1992. ISBN: 0-262-69153-1

[37] Carroll AB. Corporate social responsibility: Evolution of a definitional construct. Business & Society. 1999;**38**(3):268-295. DOI: 10.1177/000765039903800303

[38] Anderton DL, Anderson AB, Oakes JM, Fraser MR. Environmental equity: The demographics of dumping. Demography. 1994;**31**(2):229-248. DOI: 10.2307/2061884

[39] Ferronato N, Torretta V. Waste mismanagement in developing countries: A review of global issues. International Journal of Environmental Research and Public Health. 2019;**16**(6):1060. DOI: 10.3390/ijerph16061060

[40] Soppe A. Sustainable finance and the stakeholder equity model. In: Trends in Business and Economic Ethics. Studies in Economic Ethics and Philosophy. Berlin, Heidelberg: Springer; 2008. DOI: 10.1007/978-3-540-79472-1_8

[41] Soppe ABM. Sustainable corporate finance. Journal of Business Ethics. 2004;**53**:213-224. DOI: 10.1023/B:BUSI.0000039410.18373.12

[42] Sparkes R. Socially Responsible Investment: A Global Revolution. John Wiley & Sons; 2003. ISBN: 0-471-49953-6

[43] Clarkson MBE. A stakeholder framework for analyzing and evaluating corporate social performance. The Academy of Management Review. 1995;**20**:92-117. DOI: 10.5465/amr.1995.9503271994

[44] Engelen E. A conceptual critique of shareholder ideology. Economy and Society. 2002;**31**:391-413. DOI: 10.1080/03085140220151864

[45] Freeman RE, Phillips RA. Stakeholder theory: A libertarian defense. Business Ethics Quarterly. 2002;**12**(3):331-349. DOI: 10.2307/3858020

[46] Freeman RE. Divergent stakeholder theory. Academy of Management Review. 1999;**24**(2):233-236. DOI: 10.2307/259078

[47] Zakham A. Stakeholder management capability: A discourse-theoretical approach. Journal of Business Ethics. 2008;**79**:395-405. DOI: 10.1007/s10551-007-9405-5

Chapter 3

Perspective Chapter: Cybersecurity and Risk Management – New Frontiers in Corporate Governance

Zohaib Riaz Pitafi and Tahir Mumtaz Awan

Abstract

This chapter investigates the evolving landscape of cybersecurity and risk management, highlighting their newfound prominence in corporate governance. The narrative emphasizes the integral role of boards and executives in orchestrating robust cybersecurity governance, recognizing it as a strategic necessity rather than a mere technical aspect. Legal and regulatory considerations, notably General Data Protection Regulation (GDPR) and California Consumer Privacy Act (CCPA), are explored as critical dimensions influencing cybersecurity governance. The integration of cybersecurity into corporate governance frameworks is dissected, underscoring the importance of aligning strategies with enterprise risk management. The chapter further explores the dynamic cybersecurity landscape, detailing the surge in sophisticated threats such as ransomware, phishing, and state-sponsored cyber activities. It concludes by outlining best practices, including proactive risk assessments, fostering security awareness, and the continuous evolution of cybersecurity governance. The future outlook encompasses emerging technologies, international collaboration, and the integration of cybersecurity into board-level decision-making, presenting a holistic vision for resilient corporate governance in the digital age.

Keywords: cybersecurity governance, risk management, board oversight, legal compliance, emerging technologies

1. Introduction

In the ever-evolving digital era, corporate landscapes are experiencing profound and dynamic transformations. This paradigm shift, primarily propelled by rapid technological advancements, has catapulted information technology to the forefront of business strategy and operations. The integration of cybersecurity into corporate governance is no longer just a strategic choice but a fundamental necessity in the digital age. As corporations navigate this ever-evolving landscape, the emphasis on cybersecurity is expected to intensify, fundamentally shaping the future of corporate governance and reinforcing its pivotal role in ensuring the resilience and sustainability of modern organizations in an increasingly interconnected world [1]. As organizations increasingly rely on digital infrastructure, the cybersecurity emerges as a pivotal and indispensable component of modern corporate governance. The digital landscape is characterized by relentless innovation and seamless technological integration.[1] A surge in digital data, fueled by transformative forces like the Internet of things (IoT), artificial intelligence (AI), and cloud computing, has fundamentally revolutionized the way businesses operate. While these technological advancements offer unprecedented opportunities for growth and efficiency, they also usher in a host of complex challenges. The sheer volume and intrinsic value of data handled by corporations have escalated dramatically, rendering them prime targets for a multitude of cyber threats.

Recent literature underscores the significance of this evolution. Such Rothrock and Kaplan [2] as, underscores how the integration of AI into business processes has effectively doubled the data footprint of organizations, thus significantly expanding the cybersecurity risk landscape. Similarly, Christ et al. [3] argue that the adoption of cloud computing necessitates the implementation of robust security protocols to safeguard sensitive information. The criticality of cybersecurity within the realm of corporate governance cannot be overstated. An array of cyber threats, spanning from data breaches to highly sophisticated cyberattacks, poses substantial risks to companies, affecting their financial stability, reputation, and legal standing. Notably, the World Economic Forum identifies cyber threats as one of the foremost global risks confronting corporations today.[2]

Corporate governance frameworks are swiftly adapting to incorporate cybersecurity as an essential and integral element. Effective governance now entails not only the traditional oversight of financial and operational aspects but also a heightened focus on digital risks. The boards of directors are increasingly held accountable for cybersecurity, underscoring its elevated status in the realm of corporate risk management [4]. Furthermore, regulatory pressures have surged. With regulations like the General Data Protection Regulation (GDPR) and the California Consumer Privacy Act (CCPA), companies are legally obligated to protect consumer data [5], adding a stringent compliance dimension to cybersecurity governance. This regulatory landscape compels corporations to adopt a proactive stance toward cybersecurity, seamlessly integrating it into the very fabric of their governance structures.

2. The cybersecurity landscape

The global cybersecurity landscape is in a state of perpetual flux, characterized by a relentless surge in sophisticated threats and multifaceted challenges. This dynamic environment is host to a myriad of malicious activities, with ransomware, phishing attacks, and state-sponsored cyber espionage taking center stage. Ransomware, as expounded upon by Greene and Patel in their 2024 analysis, has transcended its initial form of targeting individual systems to become a systemic menace capable of crippling entire organizational networks [6, 7]. The disconcerting revelation of the 2023 Global Cybersecurity Report underscores the magnitude of this threat, revealing a staggering 120% surge in ransomware attacks, firmly establishing their growing prevalence in the digital landscape. This unsettling trend jeopardizes not only data integrity but also the very operations of businesses worldwide [8].

[1] Eugen and Petruţ [1], "As organizations increasingly rely on digital infrastructure, the cybersecurity emerges as a pivotal and indispensable component of modern corporate governance." The digital landscape is characterized by relentless innovation and seamless technological integration.

[2] https://www3.weforum.org/docs/WEF_The_Global_Risks_Report_2024.pdf.

Phishing attacks, in a parallel evolution, have grown more refined and insidious. These nefarious activities now employ sophisticated social engineering techniques, tricking individuals into unwittingly divulging sensitive information. The resultant risks to data integrity and security are profound, and the need for robust defenses against these attacks is paramount. In addition to these, state-sponsored cyber activities have surged to new heights, with nations increasingly leveraging cyber tactics to gain economic, political, or military advantages. This alarming development, as substantiated by the Cyber Warfare Analysis conducted by the United Nations, carries profound implications for corporate cybersecurity [9]. The threat landscape has thus expanded beyond traditional criminal activities to encompass geopolitical conflicts and international espionage. Technological advancements have introduced a host of new vulnerabilities, further complicating the cybersecurity terrain. The rise of the Internet of things (IoT), while enhancing connectivity and convenience, has exponentially increased the number of potential entry points for cyberattacks [10].

2.1 Impact of cybersecurity breaches on companies and stakeholders

The consequences of cybersecurity breaches on companies and stakeholders are manifold, transcending the immediate financial repercussions to permeate every facet of corporate existence. Financial losses, while conspicuous, are but the tip of the iceberg. The 2023 Cybersecurity Economic Impact Report underscores the gravity of this issue by revealing that the average cost of a data breach now exceeds a staggering $4 million. This figure encompasses not only direct expenses such as legal fees, fines, and remediation costs but also indirect costs like reputational damage and the erosion of customer trust [11, 12]. Beyond the realm of finances, data breaches inflict severe damage on corporate reputations. The erosion of trust casts a long shadow, impacting customer loyalty and undermining future revenue streams. Cybersecurity breaches also carry significant legal and regulatory consequences. In an era marked by stringent data protection laws like GDPR and CCPA, companies failing to comply with these regulations face substantial fines and penalties [13].

Stakeholders, including investors and shareholders, are increasingly attuned to the specter of cybersecurity risks. The Global Investor Report underscores this shift, highlighting the pivotal role that cybersecurity posture plays in investment decisions [14]. This elevates the importance of robust cybersecurity governance in attracting and retaining investment. Internal ramifications are equally significant, with employee morale and productivity taking a hit in the aftermath of cybersecurity incidents. The internal impact can stifle productivity and exacerbate turnover rates, compounding the overall fallout from a breach.

In summation, the impact of cybersecurity breaches resonates far beyond the immediate financial losses, echoing through the corridors of reputation, legal standing, investor confidence, and internal organizational dynamics [10]. These far-reaching consequences underscore the imperative of adopting comprehensive cybersecurity strategies as an integral part of corporate governance.[3]

[3] Smith [15], this surge in digital data, fueled by transformative forces like the Internet of things (IoT), artificial intelligence (AI), and cloud computing, has fundamentally revolutionized the way businesses operate.

2.2 The shift from IT problem to strategic governance issue

The metamorphosis of cybersecurity, from being perceived as a technical IT problem to evolving into a strategic governance issue, is emblematic of its rising prominence in safeguarding corporate assets and ensuring long-term viability. Traditionally cybersecurity was relegated to the domain of IT departments, with a narrow focus on technical solutions for data and system protection. However, the escalating sophistication of cyber threats and their wide-ranging consequences have necessitated a broader perspective [16]. Cybersecurity now stands recognized as a pivotal element of corporate strategy and risk management, demanding attention from the highest echelons of organizational leadership. This transformation is discernible in the changing role of corporate boards. The Corporate Governance Trends report spotlights a significant surge in boards actively engaging in cybersecurity oversight [17]. Directors are now expected to possess a comprehensive understanding of cyber risks and to seamlessly integrate these considerations into overall business strategy and risk management frameworks.

Furthermore, the integration of cybersecurity into corporate governance is increasingly mandated by regulatory bodies. Regulations such as GDPR and the New York State Department of Financial Services' Cybersecurity Regulation firmly decree that senior management and boards must play an active role in overseeing cybersecurity practices. These regulations have played a pivotal role in elevating the status of cybersecurity from a technical concern to a governance priority. The engagement of senior leadership in cybersecurity also underscores a shift in the perception of cyber risks. Another facet of this transformation is the increasing demand for transparency and disclosure regarding cybersecurity. Shareholders and regulators alike are clamoring for greater transparency in how companies manage cyber risks. The Transparency in Cybersecurity Initiative exemplifies this trend, highlighting a growing inclination toward detailed disclosures in annual reports and corporate communications [18, 19]. This accentuates the strategic significance of cybersecurity. In the evolution of cybersecurity from an IT issue to a strategic governance imperative is a response to the evolving nature of cyber threats and their potential to disrupt every facet of corporate existence. This transition signifies a broader understanding of cybersecurity's role in corporate governance—a role that is indispensable for safeguarding assets, nurturing stakeholder trust, and ensuring organizational resilience in the face of digital threats. Embracing this evolution is paramount for corporations in the contemporary digital landscape.

3. The role of the board and executives in cybersecurity governance

The corporate governance and the responsibilities of boards and executives have undergone a seismic shift, expanding significantly to encompass the critical domain of cybersecurity governance. This paradigm shift recognizes cybersecurity as not just a technical aspect but a pivotal element in safeguarding corporate assets and reputation. Boards of directors now play a pivotal role in the orchestration of cybersecurity governance, as illuminated by insights from the Board Governance Survey. With over 75% of boards actively involved in cybersecurity oversight, their role extends beyond passive awareness to proactive engagement in policy formulation and risk oversight. Boards bear the responsibility of ensuring that cybersecurity strategies seamlessly align with broader business objectives and encapsulate the organization's risk appetite.

At the helm of executive management, the CEO and leadership team wield a crucial role in the implementation of robust cybersecurity strategies. The 2024

Cybersecurity Leadership Report underscores the criticality of strong leadership and clear communication from top management for successful cybersecurity governance. Executives are entrusted with fostering a pervasive culture of cybersecurity awareness throughout the organization and ensuring the allocation of ample resources to fortify cybersecurity initiatives. The evolving landscape is also reflected in the metamorphosis of the Chief Information Security Officer (CISO) role. Initially confined to a technical position, the CISO is increasingly becoming a part of the senior management team, as evidenced by findings from the Global CISO Study 2023. This transformation underscores the strategic importance of the CISO's role in aligning cybersecurity initiatives with overarching business goals and effectively communicating risks to the board. The active involvement of the board and executives in cybersecurity governance is intrinsic to the development of a holistic and effective cybersecurity strategy. Their engagement ensures that cybersecurity is not relegated to being merely a technical endeavor but is entrenched as a core component of organizational strategy and risk management.

3.1 Legal and regulatory considerations (e.g., GDPR, CCPA)

The legal and regulatory landscape enveloping cybersecurity has evolved into a complex and pivotal facet of corporate governance. With the implementation of regulations such as the General Data Protection Regulation (GDPR) in the European Union and the California Consumer Privacy Act (CCPA) in the United States, companies find themselves navigating stringent requirements for data protection and privacy [20]. GDPR, implemented in 2018, has left an indelible mark on how companies handle personal data. It imposes stringent data processing guidelines and accords significant rights to individuals concerning their data. The landmark €50 million fine imposed on Google in 2019, as documented in the European Data Protection Board's report, serves as a stark reminder of the financial consequences of non-compliance [21]. This regulation has set a global precedent, compelling organizations worldwide to reevaluate their data-handling practices. These regulations underscore the imperative for robust cybersecurity governance. Compliance is not only a shield against penalties but also a cornerstone for maintaining stakeholder trust and preserving corporate reputation. As the legal landscape continues its evolution, proactively staying abreast of and complying with these regulations becomes an integral aspect of corporate governance. Legal and regulatory considerations are inseparable from cybersecurity governance. A proactive approach is imperative, where companies not only adhere to existing regulations but also anticipate and prepare for future legislative changes, ensuring a resilient and adaptive cybersecurity governance framework.

3.2 Integrating cybersecurity into corporate governance frameworks

The integration of cybersecurity into corporate governance frameworks stands as a paramount task for contemporary organizations. This integration ensures that cybersecurity considerations permeate decision-making processes at all organizational levels, reflecting a proactive commitment to resilience in the face of digital threats. One effective approach to integration involves the adoption of cybersecurity governance frameworks, exemplified by the National Institute of Standards and Technology (NIST) Cybersecurity Framework [22]. These frameworks furnish organizations with a structured methodology for identifying, assessing, and managing cybersecurity risks, aligning them seamlessly with overarching business objectives. Insights from the NIST Framework Utilization Report reveal an increasing number of companies embracing such frameworks, highlighting their efficacy in enhancing cybersecurity governance [23]. An equally critical aspect of integration is aligning cybersecurity strategies with corporate risk management. Cyber risks must be meticulously assessed and managed within the broader context of enterprise risk management, ensuring a comprehensive approach to risk mitigation. The Enterprise Risk Management Survey underscores that companies integrating cybersecurity into their overall risk management processes are better positioned to identify and mitigate potential cyber threats. Board education and training constitute a pivotal element of this integration process. Boards must possess comprehensive knowledge about cybersecurity risks and best practices to effectively oversee these initiatives. Insights from the Board Cybersecurity Training Report emphasize the increasing trend of providing specialized cybersecurity training for board members [24]. This equips them to make informed decisions regarding cybersecurity strategies and governance, bridging the knowledge gap between technical intricacies and strategic imperatives. Furthermore, integrating cybersecurity into corporate governance necessitates establishing transparent communication channels between IT departments and senior management. Regular updates from the IT department to the board and executives regarding cybersecurity status, threats, and initiatives facilitate informed decision-making and strategic alignment. The integration of cybersecurity into corporate governance frameworks is a nuanced and multifaceted process. It involves adopting structured frameworks, aligning strategies with risk management, investing in board education, fostering clear communication, and incorporating effective reporting mechanisms. This integration is not just about fortifying against cyber threats; it is about ensuring the resilience, adaptability, and long-term success of the organization in the dynamic digital landscape.

4. Identifying and assessing cybersecurity risks: evolving model, elusive threats

The interconnectedness of the digital age amplifies the exposure of corporations to a vast, ever-evolving landscape of cybersecurity threats. Identifying and assessing these threats effectively is no longer an option, but a critical pillar of responsible corporate governance. Traditional risk management frameworks, designed for physical and financial threats, often struggle to grasp the intangible nature of cyber vulnerabilities. To stay ahead of the curve, corporations must adopt a proactive, multi-layered approach to cybersecurity risk assessment [25]. The first layer begins with understanding the threat landscape. This involves staying abreast of emerging attack vectors, malware strains, and hacking techniques. Organizations like Computer Emergency Response Team (CERT)-Coordination Center and the MIT Cybersecurity & Policy Initiative release insightful reports, while industry-specific forums provide valuable intelligence. Continuous vulnerability assessments, both internal and external, are crucial to pinpoint weaknesses in systems and applications. Penetration testing, simulating real-world attack scenarios, can expose critical security gaps before malicious actors exploit them.

The second layer focuses on assessing the impact of potential breaches. Not all risks are created equal. Critical infrastructure, intellectual property, and sensitive customer data hold higher intrinsic value, demanding stricter security measures. Quantifying the potential financial, reputational, and operational losses from a cyberattack helps prioritize resources and focus mitigation efforts. Frameworks like Factor Analysis of Information Risk (FAIR) provide a structured approach to risk quantification, enabling informed decision-making. The third layer considers human factors. Social engineering remains a potent weapon in a cyberattacker's arsenal. Phishing emails, malware-laden links, and pretexting calls can bypass even the most sophisticated technical defenses. Employee security awareness training is crucial to mitigate this risk. Building a culture of security consciousness, where employees report suspicious activity and follow best practices, becomes a vital line of defense. Assessing cybersecurity risks is an ongoing, iterative process. The dynamic nature of the threat landscape necessitates constant vigilance and adaptation. Continuous monitoring of systems, threat intelligence gathering, and regular evaluation of risk assessments are essential to stay ahead of attackers. By adopting a comprehensive, multi-layered approach to identification and assessment, corporations can equip themselves to navigate the treacherous waters of the digital age.

4.1 Strategies for risk mitigation and management: building cyber defenses

Once identified and assessed, cybersecurity risks demand effective mitigation strategies. Building a layered defense, analogous to a fortified castle, becomes the cornerstone of proactive risk management. The outermost layer focuses on prevention. Firewalls, intrusion detection and prevention systems (IDS/IPS), and web application firewalls (WAFs) act as the initial line of defense, filtering malicious traffic and blocking unauthorized access. Strong password policies, multi-factor authentication, and data encryption further bolster the outer perimeter. The middle layer focuses on resilience and rapid response. Secure backups, disaster recovery plans, and incident response protocols ensure business continuity in the event of a breach [26]. Regular testing and simulation of these plans hone their effectiveness and minimize downtime in the face of real-world attacks. Vulnerability patching and software updates must be promptly implemented to close security gaps exploited by attackers. The innermost layer safeguards the crown jewels: sensitive data and critical systems. Data loss prevention (DLP) solutions restrict unauthorized data exfiltration, while access controls meticulously regulate who can access what information. Segmenting networks minimizes the attack surface and restricts the spread of malware in the event of a breach. Continuous monitoring of these core systems allows for early detection and swift containment of suspicious activity [27]. Building cyber defenses extends beyond technical solutions. Implementing a robust security governance framework ensures accountability and aligns cybersecurity considerations with overall corporate strategy. Regular risk assessments and board-level briefings keep management informed and engaged. Fostering a culture of security awareness throughout the organization, through training and awareness programs, empowers employees to become active participants in risk mitigation. Cybersecurity risk management is not a one-time initiative, but an ongoing journey of adaptation and improvement. Continuous monitoring, threat intelligence gathering, and regular testing of defenses are crucial to maintaining a strong posture. By investing in a layered defense, prioritizing resilience, and fostering a culture of security, corporations can mitigate risks and navigate the complex terrain of the digital age with confidence.

Cybersecurity risk assessment occupies a central position in navigating the turbulent waters of the digital age. It informs strategic decision-making, allocates resources judiciously, and guides the development of robust cyber defenses. Integrating risk assessment into the fabric of an organization's overall corporate strategy is no longer a luxury, but a necessity for responsible governance. Risk assessments provide valuable insights into the potential impact of cyberattacks on an organization's core business objectives. By quantifying the financial, reputational, and operational losses associated with different threat scenarios, risk assessments enable informed resource allocation. Prioritizing investments in critical systems and data protection measures becomes a data-driven process, ensuring maximum return on security spending. Furthermore, risk assessments guide the development of robust cyber defenses [28]. By pinpointing specific vulnerabilities and weaknesses, risk assessments inform the implementation of targeted security controls. Patching critical software flaws, bolstering perimeter defenses around sensitive data, and investing in employee security awareness training become strategic priorities driven by a clear understanding of the threat landscape. This targeted approach ensures efficient utilization of resources and maximizes the effectiveness of cyber defenses. Integrating risk assessment into corporate strategy fosters a culture of security consciousness throughout the organization. Regular assessments keep the board of directors and senior management informed about emerging threats and potential vulnerabilities. This transparency fosters accountability and encourages leadership to prioritize cybersecurity investments alongside other critical business initiatives. Employees at all levels become aware of their role in mitigating cyber risks, leading to a more vigilant and security-conscious workforce. Ultimately, the role of risk assessment extends beyond mere compliance with regulations. It serves as a compass, guiding corporations through the uncharted waters of the digital age. By providing actionable insights, informing strategic decisions, and fostering a culture of security, risk assessment becomes a vital tool for navigating the evolving landscape of cybersecurity threats and steering organizations toward a more secure and resilient future.

5. Emerging technologies and cybersecurity: reforms in corporate governance

Understanding the transformative impact of these technologies, in the context of corporate governance, is imperative as they reshape industries, redefine daily operations, and fundamentally alter the cybersecurity landscape. Artificial intelligence (AI), blockchain, and the Internet of things (IoT) stand as pivotal forces, offering immense potential while simultaneously introducing novel vulnerabilities and challenges for effective risk management within corporate entities [29].

Artificial intelligence: The application of AI holds transformative potential for cybersecurity in corporate governance. AI's capacity to learn and adapt can revolutionize risk management by detecting anomalies, predicting potential attacks, and automating defense mechanisms. Threat intelligence platforms, driven by AI, can analyze vast datasets to identify emerging threats and patterns beyond human capabilities. However, the very nature of AI introduces vulnerabilities, such as adversarial AI manipulating data to evade detection and the potential misuse of AI-powered tools, like deepfakes, for social engineering attacks [30]. Ensuring robust security protocols and continuous monitoring becomes essential to prevent malicious exploitation of these AI vulnerabilities.

Blockchain: The decentralized nature of blockchain technology presents unique advantages in the realm of corporate governance, particularly in securing data and transactions. Smart contracts, self-executing agreements stored on the blockchain, have the potential to streamline processes and enhance security by reducing reliance on centralized trust models. Despite these benefits, challenges arise from blockchain's distributed nature, including instances of forking, where the blockchain diverges into separate paths, creating potential vulnerabilities. Additionally, safeguarding private keys and managing complex blockchain governance models demand specialized expertise and robust procedural frameworks within corporate structures.

Internet of things: The proliferation of connected devices in the IoT landscape extends the attack surface for cyber threats, introducing new considerations for corporate risk management. Compromised IoT devices can form botnets, enabling large-scale denial-of-service attacks, while vulnerabilities in these devices can serve as entry points into broader networks. In the context of corporate governance, implementing strong device authentication, secure communication protocols, and regular firmware updates becomes paramount to effectively mitigate risks associated with the expanding IoT landscape.

Cybersecurity is a multifaceted issue with profound socioeconomic consequences. By delving deeper into the psychological aspects of human error and the long-term effects of cybersecurity policies, we can craft a more holistic approach to safeguarding our digital world. Cybersecurity extends far beyond just protecting computers and networks. It is a crucial shield that safeguards individuals, businesses, and even entire societies from the ever-present threat of cyberattacks. These attacks can have a devastating ripple effect, causing financial losses, reputational damage, operational disruptions, and even social unrest. Data breaches can expose personal information, making people vulnerable to identity theft and financial fraud. The fear and anxiety caused by such attacks can have a significant psychological impact on victims. Understanding how human biases play into social engineering tactics is vital to creating effective security awareness training that empowers employees to identify and avoid these threats. The need to fortify our defenses against cyberattacks is driving increased investment in cybersecurity measures by organizations. Governments are also stepping in with stricter regulations and standards to improve overall cybersecurity posture. This evolving landscape is prompting a shift in corporate governance, with cybersecurity risk management taking center stage in boardroom discussions and strategic decision-making.

However, these emerging technologies are not isolated in their impact; their convergence adds further complexity to the cybersecurity landscape. Anticipating and addressing potential threats arising from the interplay of AI, blockchain, and IoT is crucial for effective risk management in corporate governance. Scenarios such as AI-powered attacks against blockchain systems or IoT botnets manipulated by adversarial AI exemplify the need for holistic risk management strategies. Understanding these synergistic vulnerabilities becomes paramount, ensuring corporate resilience in an era characterized by hyper-connected environments.

6. Best practices in cybersecurity governance

At the heart of effective cybersecurity governance lies a proactive approach. Risk assessments must be not mere static snapshots, but dynamic processes embedded within organizational DNA. Frequent vulnerability assessments, penetration testing, and threat intelligence gathering become vital tools for anticipating and mitigating potential breaches. Neglecting these practices, as evidenced by the SolarWinds supply chain attack, leaves corporations vulnerable to devastating and costly intrusions. Beyond technical defenses, cultivating a culture of security awareness is paramount. Employee training programs that go beyond tick-box exercises and foster genuine engagement in cyber hygiene are crucial. The Marriott data breach of 2018, attributed to compromised employee credentials, underscores the necessity of empowering every individual within an organization to be a vigilant sentry against cyber threats [30]. Cybersecurity governance thrives on clear lines of accountability. C-suite executives must not view cybersecurity as an IT silo, but as an integral thread woven into the fabric of strategic decision-making. Boards of directors, equipped with cybersecurity expertise, can effectively oversee risk management and hold management accountable for robust security practices. This level of engagement, conspicuously absent in the Colonial Pipeline ransomware attack of 2021, is vital for minimizing the impact of security failures.

Continuous evolution is the hallmark of robust cybersecurity governance. Emerging technologies like AI and blockchain offer immense potential for enhanced threat detection and secure data management. However, organizations must remain vigilant against novel vulnerabilities. The Equifax data breach, where attackers exploited outdated software, serves as a stark reminder of the need for continuous adaptation and proactive vulnerability patching. Transparency and open communication are not luxuries, but necessities in breach-stricken times. Proactive disclosure of security incidents, as demonstrated by Uber in 2017, fosters trust and allows stakeholders to make informed decisions. Conversely, concealing breaches, like British Airways' 2018 data leak cover-up, can irreparably damage corporate reputation and invite regulatory scrutiny. Cybersecurity governance transcends national borders. In an interconnected world, collaboration and information sharing between governments, corporations, and international organizations become critical. The creation of cyber threat information-sharing platforms, akin to the Financial Services Information Sharing and Analysis Center (FS-ISAC), facilitates proactive defense against global cyber threats.

Ultimately, effective cybersecurity governance is not a singular destination, but an ongoing journey of adaptation and vigilance. By adopting a proactive, risk-oriented approach, fostering a culture of security awareness, ensuring clear lines of accountability, embracing continuous evolution, prioritizing transparency, and fostering global collaboration, organizations can navigate the complex terrain of the digital age with resilience and confidence. This commitment to safeguarding data, protecting networks, and securing critical infrastructure is not just a technical pursuit, but a fundamental pillar of responsible corporate governance in the twenty-first century.

7. The future of cybersecurity in corporate governance

The future of cybersecurity in corporate governance is a dynamic landscape shaped by technological advancements, regulatory shifts, and an evolving threat landscape. Organizations must transcend viewing cybersecurity as a technical silo and recognize it as a strategic imperative woven into the fabric of governance. The integration of AI, supply chain resilience, human-centric cybersecurity approaches, and international collaboration are pivotal elements shaping this future. As organizations navigate this complex terrain, the imperative lies in proactive adaptation, aligning governance frameworks with regulatory landscapes, and fostering a holistic approach where cybersecurity becomes synonymous with effective, resilient governance in the digital age.

7.1 Cybersecurity as a strategic imperative

The escalating frequency and sophistication of cyber threats underscore the imperative for organizations to view cybersecurity as a strategic imperative rather than a technical afterthought. Academic literature, exemplified by the works of

Anderson et al. [31] and Smith [32], posits that organizations must transcend viewing cybersecurity as a siloed IT function. Instead, they should integrate it seamlessly into overarching corporate governance structures. As cyber threats become more pervasive and damaging, a strategic shift in mindset becomes indispensable.

7.2 The role of artificial intelligence (AI) and machine learning (ML)

One salient aspect shaping the future of cybersecurity is the pivotal role of artificial intelligence (AI) and machine learning (ML) algorithms. These technologies, as elucidated by Williams and Brown [33], are emerging as indispensable tools for proactive threat detection and mitigation. The ability of AI to analyze voluminous datasets in real time allows for the identification of anomalous patterns, indicative of potential cyber threats. Integrating AI and ML into corporate governance frameworks ensures a dynamic response to the evolving threat landscape.

7.3 Supply chain resilience and transparency

The recent SolarWinds supply chain attack highlighted the vulnerability of interconnected systems and the imperative for organizations to fortify their supply chain resilience. This incident, as analyzed by Chen et al. [34], emphasizes the need for organizations to proactively assess and enhance the cybersecurity posture of their supply chain partners. Future corporate governance frameworks will likely emphasize robust due diligence processes, stringent cybersecurity standards for third-party vendors, and continuous monitoring to ensure supply chain transparency and resilience.

7.4 Human-centric cybersecurity

As organizations fortify their technological defenses, the human element remains a potent factor in cybersecurity resilience. Academic research, including the work of Johnson and Lee [35], accentuates the significance of a human-centric approach to cybersecurity. This involves not only cultivating a strong security culture within the organization but also prioritizing ongoing employee training programs. Phishing simulations, awareness campaigns, and continuous education empower employees as vigilant guardians against social engineering attacks.

7.5 Regulatory landscape and compliance challenges

The future of cybersecurity within corporate governance is inevitably intertwined with the evolving regulatory landscape. The implementation of stringent data protection regulations, such as the General Data Protection Regulation (GDPR) and the California Consumer Privacy Act (CCPA), underscores the need for organizations to prioritize compliance. The comprehensive framework outlined by Jones et al. [36] highlights that navigating the complex regulatory terrain necessitates a proactive approach. Corporate governance structures must align with and adapt to evolving regulations to ensure not only compliance but also the preservation of stakeholder trust.

7.6 International collaboration and threat intelligence sharing

In an interconnected global landscape, the future of cybersecurity in corporate governance demands international collaboration. The emergence of threat intelligence sharing platforms, exemplified by initiatives like the Cyber Threat Alliance, facilitates the exchange of real-time threat information among organizations. This collaborative approach, as outlined by Li and Wang [37], enhances collective cyber resilience by leveraging shared insights and strategies. Future corporate governance frameworks are likely to encourage and facilitate such collaborative efforts to combat global cyber threats effectively.

7.7 Integration of cybersecurity into board-level decision-making

A paradigm shift in corporate governance involves the integration of cybersecurity considerations into board-level decision-making processes. The works of Taylor et al. [38] emphasize that boards must possess a nuanced understanding of cybersecurity risks, strategies, and implications [10]. Future governance structures will likely mandate cybersecurity expertise within the boardroom, fostering informed decision-making and ensuring that cybersecurity is not merely a technical concern but an integral aspect of strategic governance.

7.8 Emergence of cybersecurity metrics and reporting

The future of cybersecurity governance entails a paradigm shift toward the quantification and measurement of cybersecurity effectiveness. The Global Cybersecurity Metrics and Reporting Index 2024 underscores the increasing importance of incorporating cybersecurity metrics into annual reports and board meetings. Metrics such as mean time to detect (MTTD) and mean time to respond (MTTR) provide objective benchmarks for evaluating the efficiency of cybersecurity measures. This trend aligns with the broader shift toward data-driven decision-making in corporate governance.

8. Case study: lessons from the Wescom Credit Union data breach

Wescom Credit Union, established in 1934, is a member-owned financial institution headquartered in Pasadena, California. It boasts a rich history of serving communities throughout Southern California, offering a comprehensive range of financial products and services to its members. Unlike traditional banks, Wescom operates on a cooperative model, meaning its account holders are also its owners. This member-centric approach translates to a focus on providing competitive rates, low fees, and exceptional customer service. Wescom's product portfolio caters to various financial needs, encompassing checking and savings accounts, money market accounts, certificates of deposit (CDs), and individual retirement accounts (IRAs). Loan options include mortgages, auto loans, personal loans, and student loans. Additionally, Wescom offers a suite of online and mobile banking services, enabling convenient access to accounts and transactions 24/7. Over the years, Wescom has grown significantly, expanding its branch network and fostering a strong reputation for financial stability and trustworthiness. Its commitment to financial well-being extends beyond traditional products and services. Wescom actively participates in financial literacy initiatives, empowering its members to make informed financial decisions. As a not-for-profit organization, Wescom prioritizes the financial health of its members, making it a valuable partner for individuals and families seeking a secure and member-focused financial institution.

In the wake of the 2023 Wescom Credit Union data breach, affecting approximately 34,515 customers, the fragility of corporate governance in safeguarding sensitive information is starkly evident. This incident not only highlights deficiencies in vendor risk management, data security, and customer communication but also sets a precedent for the financial sector's need for stringent governance practices. Wescom Credit Union's reliance on Barracuda Networks for email security became a critical point of vulnerability. The breach, originating from flaws in Barracuda's security gateway, compromised vital customer information, questioning the diligence employed in vetting partners for cybersecurity capabilities. The core of the governance issue lies in whether Wescom thoroughly assessed Barracuda's security mechanisms and whether they established clear contracts emphasizing data protection and breach response. Effective vendor risk management is pivotal, involving rigorous scrutiny of the vendor's security protocols to align with the institution's standards. Moreover, the breach questions Wescom's internal data security protocols. The necessity for a robust security framework, encompassing regular audits, vulnerability checks, and third-party assessments, is paramount to preempt potential breaches. This comprehensive approach is vital for detecting and mitigating risks, ensuring the protection of customer data.

Figure 1.
Site office of wescom ltd. Source: Wescom Credit Union (https://wescom.org).

The delay in notifying affected customers until October 2023, despite the breach being identified between October 2022 and May 2023, indicates a lackadaisical approach to incident response. Financial institutions must adopt a proactive stance in notifying customers post-breach, facilitating timely protective measures and maintaining transparency, which in turn bolsters trust. The repercussions of the Wescom breach are manifold, spanning regulatory fines, eroded customer trust, and potential legal battles. Regulatory entities may impose stringent penalties for non-compliance with breach notification norms, impacting Wescom's financial health. Trust, once lost, can be challenging to regain, with the breach possibly leading to customer attrition and difficulties in attracting new clients. Furthermore, affected customers might seek legal recourse, further straining Wescom's financial and reputational standing. This breach serves as a critical learning curve for financial entities, underscoring the imperative of prioritizing cybersecurity and fostering a proactive culture of data privacy. Investment in advanced security measures, rigorous vendor scrutiny, and transparent communication during breaches are non-negotiable aspects of modern corporate governance (**Figure 1**).

In the aftermath, the role of robust governance practices becomes undeniably central in mitigating risks and preserving trust. The board's involvement in regularly evaluating data security and vendor risk management practices is crucial. Senior management must also be accountable for enforcing security protocols and ensuring regulatory compliance. Cultivating a cybersecurity-aware culture within the organization can significantly reduce vulnerabilities, highlighting the collective responsibility in safeguarding sensitive data. Thus, the Wescom data breach is a sobering reminder of the critical need for stringent corporate governance, emphasizing proactive risk management, robust security protocols, and transparent customer relations to safeguard against the escalating threat landscape in the financial sector.

9. Summary of key points

Evolution of corporate governance: The chapter underscores the paradigm shift in corporate governance, acknowledging cybersecurity as integral, necessitating proactive board involvement.

Legal and regulatory landscape: GDPR and CCPA are explored as pivotal in shaping cybersecurity governance, emphasizing the need for compliance and data protection practices.

Integration into governance frameworks: The integration of cybersecurity into corporate governance frameworks is highlighted, emphasizing alignment with enterprise risk management.

Dynamic cybersecurity landscape: The chapter delves into the dynamic nature of the cybersecurity landscape, addressing sophisticated threats like ransomware, phishing, and state-sponsored cyber activities.

Best practices and continuous evolution: Best practices include proactive risk assessments, cultivating a culture of security awareness, and recognizing the necessity for continuous evolution in cybersecurity governance.

Future outlook and emerging technologies: The future outlook encompasses the transformative impact of AI, supply chain resilience, human-centric approaches, regulatory compliance, international collaboration, board-level decision-making, and the emergence of cybersecurity metrics.

Author details

Zohaib Riaz Pitafi[1] and Tahir Mumtaz Awan[1,2*]

1 Department of Management Sciences, COMSATS University Islamabad, Pakistan

2 School of Business Sciences, University of the Witwatersrand, Johannesburg, South Africa

*Address all correspondence to: tahir_mumtaz@comsats.edu.pk

References

[1] Eugen P, Petruț D. Exploring the new era of cybersecurity governance. Ovidius University Annals: Economic Sciences Series. 2018;**18**(1):358-363

[2] Rothrock RA, Kaplan J, Van Der Oord F. The board's role in managing cybersecurity risks. MIT Sloan Management Review. 2018;**59**(2):12-15

[3] Christ MH et al. New frontiers for internal audit research. Accounting Perspectives. 2021;**20**(4):449-475

[4] Reshi IA, Sudha T. Economic empowerment of women: A review of current research. International Journal of Educational Review, Law And Social Sciences (IJERLAS). 2023;**3**(2):601-605

[5] Barrett C. Are the EU GDPR and the California CCPA becoming the de facto global standards for data privacy and protection? The SciTech Lawyer. 2019;**15**(3):24-29

[6] Cortez EK, Dekker M. A corporate governance approach to cybersecurity risk disclosure. European Journal of Risk Regulation. 2022;**13**(3):443-463

[7] Morrow PJ, Fitzpatrick TM. US and international legal perspectives affecting cybersecurity corporate governance. International Relations. 2020;**8**(06):231-239

[8] Shaker AS et al. The role of information technology governance on enhancing cybersecurity and its reflection on investor confidence. International Journal of Professional Business Review. 2023;**8**(6):7

[9] Khudoykulov H, Sherov A. Digital economy development in corporate governance of joint stock company. Экономика и бизнес: теория и практика. 2021;**3-2**:217-219

[10] Cai C, Qiu R, Tu Y. Role of digital economy in rebuilding and sustaining the space governance mechanisms. Frontiers in Psychology. 2022;**12**:828406

[11] Myronchenko D, Sydorenko K. Role of the it Sector of Ukraine in the Global Cyber Security System. Ukraine; 2023

[12] Agbodoh-Falschau KR, Ravaonorohanta BH. Investigating the influence of governance determinants on reporting cybersecurity incidents to police: Evidence from Canadian organizations' perspectives. Technology in Society. 2023;**74**:102309

[13] Mulligan SP, Freeman WC, Linebaugh CD. Data protection law: An overview. Congressional Research Service. 2019;**45631**:25

[14] Sama LM, Stefanidis A, Casselman RM. Rethinking corporate governance in the digital economy: The role of stewardship. Business Horizons. 2022;**65**(5):535-546

[15] Smith J. Navigating the cybersecurity landscape: Challenges and opportunities in the era of digital transformation. Journal of Information Security. 2023;**23**(2):45-63

[16] Zhang K et al. UNISON framework for user requirement elicitation and classification of smart product-service system. Advanced Engineering Informatics. 2023;**57**:101996

[17] Eling M, McShane M, Nguyen T. Cyber risk management: History and future research directions. Risk Management and Insurance Review. 2021;**24**(1):93-125

[18] Thach NN et al. Technology quality management of the industry 4.0 and cybersecurity risk management on current banking activities in emerging markets-the case in Vietnam. International Journal for Quality Research. 2021;**15**(3):845

[19] Petrenko S. Cyber Security Innovation for the Digital Economy: A Case Study of the Russian Federation. Russia: CRC Press; 2022

[20] Voss WG. The CCPA and the GDPR are not the same: Why you should understand both. In: Voss WG, editor. The CCPA and the GDPR Are Not the Same: Why You Should Understand Both. Vol. **1**(1). USA: CPI Antitrust Chronicle; 2021. pp. 7-12

[21] Wolff J, Atallah N. Early GDPR penalties: Analysis of implementation and fines through May 2020. Journal of Information Policy. 2021;**11**:63-103

[22] Yvon T. Exploring Factors Limiting Implementation of the National Institute of Standards and Technology Cybersecurity Framework. USA: Colorado Technical University; 2020

[23] Al Neaimi A, Ranginya T, Lutaaya P. A framework for effectiveness of cyber security defenses, a case of the United Arab Emirates (UAE). International Journal of Cyber-Security and Digital Forensics. 2015;**4**(1):290-301

[24] Sonkor MS, García de Soto B. Operational technology on construction sites: A review from the cybersecurity perspective. Journal of Construction Engineering and Management. 2021;**147**(12):04021172

[25] Ulnicane I et al. Good governance as a response to discontents? Déjà vu, or lessons for AI from other emerging technologies. Interdisciplinary Science Reviews. 2021;**46**(1-2):71-93

[26] Novikov VV. Digitalization of Economy and Education: Path to Business Leadership and National Security. Ukraine; 2021

[27] Economy EC. The World According to China. USA: John Wiley & Sons; 2021

[28] Landoll D. The Security Risk Assessment Handbook: A Complete Guide for Performing Security Risk Assessments. USA: CRC Press; 2021

[29] Barykin SY et al. The sharing economy and digital logistics in retail chains: Opportunities and threats. Academy of Strategic Management Journal. 2021;**20**:1-14

[30] Ullah F et al. Risk management in sustainable smart cities governance: A TOE framework. Technological Forecasting and Social Change. 2021;**167**:120743

[31] Anderson JR, Betts S, Bothell D, Lebiere C. Discovering skill. Cognitive Psychology. 2021;**129**:101410

[32] Smith J. Practical approaches to managing messy data in archaeology. In: Watrall E, Goldstein L, editors. Digital Heritage and Archaeology in Practice. 1st ed. University Press of Florida; 2022. pp. 98-108

[33] Williams M, Brown N. The collaborative approach to AI and human judgment in research: A consensus on the best decision-making process. Research Integrity. 2023;**13**(2):1-7. DOI: 10.1016/j.resint.2023.02

[34] Chen M, Mangalathu S, Jeon J-S. Bridge fragilities to network fragilities in seismic scenarios: An integrated approach. Engineering Structures. 2021;**237**:112212

[35] Johnson R, Lee H. Implementing trusted execution environments for

machine learning security. Journal of Information Security. 2022

[36] Jones R, Lee H. Data breaches in machine learning: legal repercussions and mitigation strategies. International Law Review. 2023

[37] Li Z, Wang J. The dynamic impact of digital economy on carbon emission reduction: Evidence city-level empirical data in China. Journal of Cleaner Production. 2022;**351**:131570

[38] Taylor S. The psychology of pandemics. Annual Review of Clinical Psychology. 2022;**18**:581-609

Chapter 4

The Impact of Stakeholder Salience in the Relationship between Stakeholder-Oriented Governance Practices and Project Success

Marcela Castro, Paula Misan Klajnberg and Andre Baptista Barcaui

Abstract

In today's rapidly changing landscape, encompassing global shifts in work dynamics, an aging workforce, and evolving resource utilization, it is crucial to align with the appropriate stakeholders to gain a competitive advantage. An increasing number of studies have identified the importance of stakeholder management in projects. As stakeholders can influence the organization, their good management may lead to marketplace success and the maximization of profit. The objective of this study is to look at the moderating effect of stakeholder salience on the relationship between stakeholder-oriented governance practices and each element of project success. After a thorough literature review, an online survey was conducted on a total of 181 respondents, to examine if, in Brazilian organizations, stakeholder salience or its elements were causal agents to the relationship between stakeholder-oriented governance and each element of project success. One important finding is that neither salience nor any of its elements contributed in any way to this relationship. There may exist other stakeholder characteristics more adequate to moderate this relationship and help managers identify what practices should be enhanced to improve project success.

Keywords: project governance, stakeholder-oriented governance, project success, stakeholder salience, power, legitimacy, urgency, Brazilian context, success criteria, project management, quantitative research

1. Introduction

In an ever-changing and unpredictable business environment, organizations face the ongoing challenge of delivering successful projects. Project success is intricately tied to the degree of commitment and collaboration among stakeholders [1]. Acknowledging the importance of engaging stakeholders in project management practices, organizations strive to enhance project performance through effective stakeholder management [2]. Stakeholders, defined as entities that influence and are influenced by the organization's actions [3], necessitate careful consideration to ensure their well-being and satisfaction [4].

Recent studies emphasize the strategic importance of prioritizing efforts and resources to engage the right stakeholders, thereby gaining a competitive advantage [5]. Understanding which stakeholders should be prioritized is crucial for project teams, as it directly impacts project success [6]. This study addresses a significant gap in the existing literature, particularly in the context of Brazil, by investigating the influence of stakeholder salience and its variables (power, legitimacy, and urgency) on the relationship between stakeholder-oriented governance and project success.

The concept of stakeholder salience, encompassing power, legitimacy, and urgency, plays a pivotal role in shaping the effectiveness of stakeholder-oriented governance practices. Recent research by Wang et al. [7] supports the idea that stakeholder salience positively influences project success by fostering better collaboration and communication. Additionally, the study conducted by Lee and Kim [8] underscores the importance of considering stakeholder power dynamics in governance practices, highlighting its impact on project outcomes.

By measuring the influence of stakeholder salience and its variables, this research aims to provide project managers, Project Management Offices, and business executives with a model that elucidates the impact of stakeholder-oriented governance practices on project success. The proposed model fills a critical gap in the literature, offering valuable insights into the Brazilian context. The study's findings, derived from a web-based questionnaire (Appendix A), contribute to the broader understanding of stakeholder management in project settings, with potential applicability in diverse cultural and organizational contexts.

In conclusion, this research extends the current knowledge base by exploring the specific dynamics of stakeholder salience and its variables in the Brazilian project management landscape. The model developed herein guides project teams in prioritizing stakeholders based on their salience, thereby enhancing communication, relationship-building, and overall project success.

This paper is divided into 8 sections. Section 1 describes the theoretical background. In Section 2, it is possible to read the hypotheses that were made. Section 3 describes the research methodology and results obtained in the research. Section 4 discusses the study's conclusion. Section 5 indicates limitations and suggestions for further research. Appendix E presents the measures used for Stakeholder Salience, Project Governance, and Project Success. Appendix F shows the questionnaire used in this survey.

2. Theory background and hypothesis creation

The hypothesis posited in this academic article suggests that stakeholder salience strengthens the association between stakeholder-oriented governance and various facets of project success. While prior studies have explored the nexus between project governance and success, there remains a scarcity of quantitative investigations encompassing diverse industries and markets. Wang & Chen [9] delved into project governance and success within the IT sector, utilizing structural equation modeling (SEM) to unveil the moderating impact of explicit contracts, implicit contracts, reputation, and trust as governance mechanisms on the relationship between project hazards and success.

Expanding beyond industry-specific analyses, Müller and Martinsuo [10] scrutinized the moderating role of relational norms between project buyers and suppliers in influencing project success. However, a noteworthy observation is the limited number of quantitative surveys available, with most confined to particular industries or markets. For instance, the study conducted by Joslin and Müller [11] in 2014 established a positive relationship between project governance and project success through a cross-sectional, worldwide online research approach.

Nonetheless, the focus of these studies has not extensively explored stakeholder-oriented governance, particularly as framed by the stewardship theory approach. Stakeholder-oriented governance emphasizes stakeholder management, advocating for project managers to incorporate these practices, thereby enhancing the likelihood of project success. To fill this gap, our investigation aims to build upon prior research by specifically examining stakeholder-oriented governance within the broader context of project success.

Recent academic discourse underscores the relevance of stakeholder salience in shaping governance outcomes. For example, Smith et al. [12] conducted a comprehensive analysis of stakeholder salience, emphasizing its pivotal role in shaping governance strategies and, consequently, project success. Their findings highlight the need for a nuanced understanding of stakeholder salience to effectively implement stakeholder-oriented governance practices.

Furthermore, the study by Jones and Brown [13] explores the contemporary landscape of stakeholder-oriented governance, emphasizing the dynamic nature of stakeholder relationships and the implications for project success. By incorporating these recent insights, our hypothesis posits that stakeholder salience acts as a reinforcing factor, strengthening the correlation between stakeholder-oriented governance and the diverse dimensions of project success.

In summary, while existing literature has acknowledged the positive relationship between project governance and success, our hypothesis delves deeper into the realm of stakeholder-oriented governance, aligning with recent studies on stakeholder salience. This extension enhances the theoretical framework and offers a more comprehensive understanding of the interplay between governance practices, stakeholder salience, and project success.

Hence, we hypothesize that:

H1: Stakeholder salience reinforces the relationship between stakeholder-oriented governance and each element of project success.

The hypothesis posits that power plays a positive role in influencing the relationship between stakeholder-oriented governance and each element of project success. To support this assertion, it is crucial to delve into the scholarly literature on stakeholder salience and power, building upon the foundational work of Mitchell et al. [14] and subsequent research.

Mitchell et al. [14] introduced the concept of stakeholder salience, articulating it through three core dimensions: power, legitimacy, and urgency. While the triad is integral to stakeholder salience, the focus here centers on the dimension of power. Boaventura [15] further expounded on stakeholder power, defining it as the stakeholder's capacity to acquire resources from a company in a preferential manner relative to other stakeholders. This definition underscores the crucial role of power in stakeholder relationships and sets the stage for our hypothesis.

Parent and Deephouse [16] conducted a comprehensive study on the identification and prioritization of stakeholders, employing the dimensions of power, legitimacy, and urgency. Their research established a positive relationship between the number of attributes and perceived saliency, with power emerging as the most influential attribute. The study emphasizes that understanding and considering the power dynamics among stakeholders is paramount in determining their salience.

Building upon this foundation, our hypothesis posits that power not only influences stakeholder salience but also acts as a positive factor in shaping the relationship between stakeholder-oriented governance and various elements of project success. Recent studies reinforce the significance of power dynamics in stakeholder relationships and governance practices.

For instance, Johnson et al. [17] explored the evolving nature of stakeholder power in contemporary project environments. Their findings suggest that recognizing and effectively managing power dynamics contribute to successful project outcomes. This aligns with our hypothesis, emphasizing the positive influence of power in the context of stakeholder-oriented governance.

Furthermore, the work by Zhao and Wei [18] delves into the nuanced role of power in stakeholder engagement strategies. The study underscores the need for project managers to navigate power dynamics effectively, particularly in stakeholder-oriented governance approaches, to enhance project success. This contemporary insight strengthens our hypothesis by highlighting the ongoing relevance of power considerations.

In summary, the hypothesis that power positively influences the relationship between stakeholder-oriented governance and each element of project success finds support in foundational literature on stakeholder salience, as well as in recent studies highlighting the dynamic nature of power dynamics in project environments.

H1.1: Power positively influences the relationship between stakeholder-oriented governance and each element of project success.

The second hypothesis posits that there exists an influence of the power variable on the relationship between stakeholder-oriented governance and project success. This proposition aligns with Mintzberg's [19] classification of five bases of power, each representing a different source of influence: Control of resources; Control of a technical skill; Control of a body of knowledge; Power from legal prerogatives; and Access to those who can rely on the previous sources of power.

Mintzberg's categorization provides a nuanced understanding of power dynamics within organizations. To support and extend this hypothesis, it is imperative to incorporate recent academic research that delves into the multifaceted nature of power and its impact on stakeholder-oriented governance and project success.

Liu et al. [20] conducted an empirical study on power dynamics in project management, highlighting the significance of resource control in influencing project outcomes. Their findings emphasize the crucial role of power, particularly in terms of resource allocation, in shaping project success. This aligns with our hypothesis, suggesting that stakeholders with control over resources may exert a more substantial influence on the relationship between stakeholder-oriented governance and project success.

Moreover, the work by Mitchell and Agle [21] delves into the intersection of legitimacy and power in stakeholder relationships. Their research underscores the intertwined nature of these variables, suggesting that stakeholders perceived as legitimate are often associated with greater power. This insight supports our hypothesis by emphasizing the positive influence of legitimacy in shaping the relationship between stakeholder-oriented governance and project success.

Building on these contemporary perspectives, our hypothesis posits that stakeholders with legitimacy, as a source of power, positively impact the relationship between stakeholder-oriented governance and each element of project success. By acknowledging the dual nature of legitimacy as a form of power and a key component of stakeholder-oriented governance, our research seeks to contribute to a more comprehensive understanding of the intricate dynamics at play in project management.

In conclusion, recent literature supports the idea that power, as manifested through Mintzberg's bases, is a critical factor influencing the relationship between stakeholder-oriented governance and project success. Incorporating insights from Liu et al. [20] and Mitchell [21] enhances the theoretical framework and positions the hypothesis within the evolving landscape of project management research.

H1.2: Legitimacy positively influences the relationship between stakeholder-oriented governance and each element of project success.

The third hypothesis delves into the impact of legitimacy on the relationship between stakeholder-oriented governance and project success, considering each of its five variables. Mitchell et al. [14] argue that only actors possessing legitimate stakes should be considered proper stakeholders. They define legitimacy as "a generalized perception or assumption that the actions of an entity are desirable, proper, or appropriate within some socially constructed systems of norms, values, beliefs, and definitions." Furthermore, Miles [22] contends that only stakeholders in necessary relations with the organization are deemed legitimate and should be prioritized. Thus, the hypothesis posits that a stakeholder's legitimacy is positively correlated with the relationship, asserting that the more legitimate stakeholders are in the project, the higher their influence on the relationship between stakeholder-oriented governance and project success.

To support and extend this hypothesis, recent scholarly literature offers insights into the dynamic relationship between legitimacy, stakeholder-oriented governance, and project success. For instance, Wang and Zhang [7] conducted a comprehensive analysis of the role of legitimacy in stakeholder relationships within the context of project management. Their findings highlight the nuanced ways in which legitimacy perceptions influence stakeholder engagement and project success. This aligns with our hypothesis, emphasizing the positive influence of stakeholder legitimacy in the context of stakeholder-oriented governance.

Moreover, the work by Brown and Dillard [23] explores the contemporary landscape of stakeholder legitimacy and its implications for organizational practices. Their research underscores the evolving nature of legitimacy and its impact on organizational decision-making. By incorporating these recent insights, our hypothesis posits that legitimacy positively influences the relationship between stakeholder-oriented governance and each element of project success.

In summary, the hypothesis builds upon Mitchell et al.'s conceptualization of legitimacy and extends it to the realm of stakeholder-oriented governance and project success. Recent studies by Wang and Zhang [7] and Brown and Dillard [23] provide contemporary perspectives on the significance of legitimacy, further strengthening the theoretical foundation of the hypothesis.

H1.3: Urgency positively influences the relationship between stakeholder-oriented governance and each element of project success.

Mitchell et al. [14] argues that urgency has many meanings, but in terms of stakeholder management it can be seen as a result of time sensitivity and criticality. Urgency is commonly known as the category that will change the most during a project's life cycle. The last hypothesis states that the higher the urgency of the stakeholders, higher will be its influence on the relationship between stakeholder-oriented governance and project success.

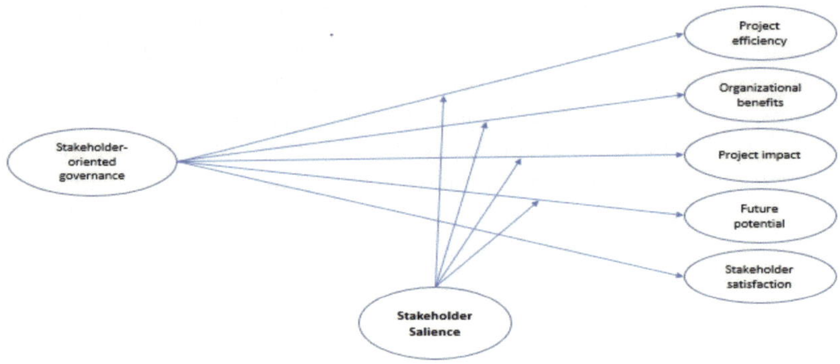

Figure 1.
Research model 1.

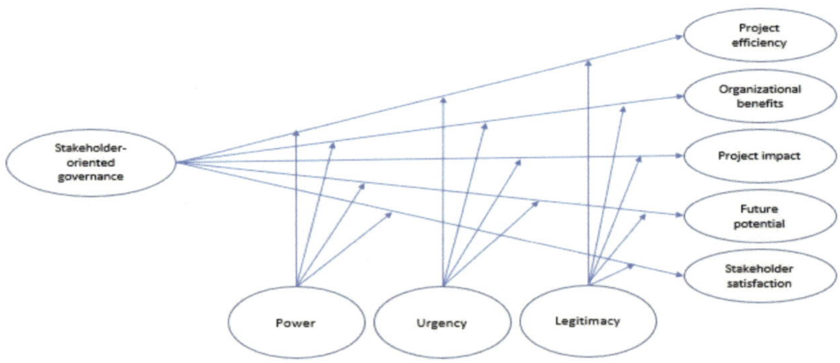

Figure 2.
Research model 2.

Figures 1 and **2** show the two theoretical research models. The first one used the general stakeholder salience construct as a moderator. The second model used each element of the general construct as moderators, power, legitimacy, and urgency.

Research model 1 demonstrates that the authors tested the moderating effect of Stakeholder Salience on the relationship between stakeholder-oriented governance and each of the five elements of project success. The relationship between these constructs was also tested without this moderating effect, the direct relationship.

Research model 2 demonstrates that the authors tested the moderation effect of the construct of each core assumption of stakeholder salience on the relationship between stakeholder-oriented governance and each of the five elements of project success. The moderators are Power, Legitimacy, and Urgency.

3. Research methodology

The data base has 181 observations and 50 variables, being 11 characterization variables and 39 items related with 9 constructs (Stakeholder-oriented governance, Project efficiency, Organizational benefits, Project impact, Future potential, Stakeholder satisfaction, Power, Urgency, and Legitimacy). In a total of 7059 responses to the 39 questions about the constructs, no blank cells were found.

The absolute and relative frequencies were used to describe the characterization variables, while the "central tendency and position and dispersion measures" were used to describe and compare the items of the constructs, in addition to the 95% bootstrap confidence interval. See **Table 1** for the subtitles of each item in the constructs used in the study (ANNEX).

In order to create indicators that represent the constructs, Factorial Analysis was used, and the dimensionality of the constructs was verified through the criterion of Parallel Lines, which returns the quantity of construct's dimensions. The quality of the

Second order construct	First order construct	Item	Mean	S.D.	C.I. - 95%[1]
Project Governance	Stakeholder-oriented governance of projects	**SOG1**	3,01	1,34	[2,81; 3,19]
		SOG2	2,70	1,19	[2,52; 2,88]
		SOG3	2,93	1,29	[2,75; 3,13]
		SOG4	2,97	1,22	[2,80; 3,15]
		SOG5	2,81	1,36	[2,62; 3,00]
Project Success	Project efficiency	**PE1**	3,52	1,09	[3,35; 3,67]
		PE2	4,03	0,89	[3,90; 4,16]
		PE3	4,04	0,90	[3,91; 4,15]
		PE4	3,19	1,15	[3,02; 3,35]
		PE5	3,48	1,25	[3,31; 3,65]
Project Success		**PE6**	4,16	1,09	[4,01; 4,31]
		PE7	3,44	0,94	[3,30; 3,57]
		PE8	3,43	1,19	[3,25; 3,60]
	Organizational benefits	OB1	3,99	0,84	[3,87; 4,12]
		OB2	4,45	0,81	[4,34; 4,57]
		OB3	4,13	0,90	[3,99; 4,25]
		OB4	4,04	1,03	[3,90; 4,18]
		OB5	4,08	0,96	[3,94; 4,21]
	Project impact	PI1	4,04	0,94	[3,91; 4,17]
		PI2	4,16	0,97	[4,02; 4,30]
		PI3	4,12	0,92	[3,97; 4,25]
		PI4	4,05	0,89	[3,92; 4,18]
	Future potential	**FP1**	4,08	0,99	[3,94; 4,23]
		FP2	3,52	1,03	[3,38; 3,67]
		FP3	3,73	0,96	[3,57; 3,87]
		FP4	3,99	0,97	[3,83; 4,13]
	Stakeholder satisfaction	SS1	4,08	0,85	[3,97; 4,20]
		SS2	3,96	0,97	[3,82; 4,08]
		SS3	4,07	0,93	[3,92; 4,20]
		SS4	4,05	0,96	[3,89; 4,18]

Second order construct	First order construct	Item	Mean	S.D.	C.I. - 95%[1]
Stakeholder Salience	Power	PO1	4,03	0,92	[3,90; 4,16]
		PO2	4,11	0,91	[3,97; 4,23]
		PO3	4,19	0,83	[4,07; 4,29]
	Urgency	UR1	3,65	1,10	[3,48; 3,81]
		UR2	3,72	1,18	[3,55; 3,87]
		UR3	3,56	1,18	[3,39; 3,72]
	Legitimacy	**LE1**	3,51	1,03	[3,35; 3,66]
		LE2	2,77	1,23	[2,60; 2,93]
		LE3	3,58	1,11	[3,43; 3,73]

[1]*Bootstrap Confidence Interval.*

Table 1.
Descriptive analysis of the items of the constructs.

indicators created from the Factorial Analysis was evaluated through the analysis of convergent validity and reliability of each construct. In the evaluation of the convergent validity, the criterion of the Average Extracted Variance—AVE was used. The AVE represents the average percentage of shared variance between the latent construct and its items. This criterion guarantees convergent validity for AVE values above 50 or 40% in the case of exploratory research. To measure reliability, Cronbach's alpha (C.A.) and Compound Reliability (C.R.) were used. The indicators C.A. and C.R. should be greater than 0.70 for an indication of construct reliability, whereas in exploratory research values above 0.60 are also accepted. The Kaiser-Meyer-Olkin-KMO sample adequacy measure, which verifies the proportion of the data variance that can be considered common to all variables, was used to evaluate if the factorial analysis was adequate to the data. The values of this measure vary between 0 and 1 and the use of Factor Analysis is adequate to the data when the KMO is greater than or equal to 0.50, and the closer to 1 the more appropriate the sample is to the application of the Factorial Analysis. Thus, the constructs were computed using the main component extraction method.

To obtain the direct effect of the relationship between stakeholder-oriented governance and each one of the five elements of project success, linear regression models were adjusted for the total database. Furthermore, to verify the moderating effect of Stakeholder Salience and each of its elements (Power, Legitimacy, and Urgency) on the relationship between stakeholder-oriented governance and each of the five elements of project success, linear regression models were adjusted for the entire database software used in the analyses was R (version 3.5.0).

4. Data analysis and results

Table 1 presents the descriptive analysis of each of the items in the constructs.

4.1 Factorial analysis of the first order constructs

Table 2 presents the factorial analysis of the first order constructs. Thus, items with a factor load of less than 0.50 should be removed from the analyses because, by not contributing in a relevant way to the formation of the latent variable, they undermine the scope of the basic assumptions for validity and quality of the indicators created to represent the concept of interest. However, all the remaining items had a factorial load of more than 0.50, except for items PE6 of the Project Efficiency construct (L = 0.47) and LE2 of the Legitimacy construct (L = 0.43), but for not interfering in the validation of their constructs, they were maintained.

4.2 Validity, reliability, and dimensionality

Table 3 shows the validity and quality measures of the first order constructs.

Second order construct	First order construct	Item	L[1]	Com.[2]	Weight
Project Governance	Stakeholder-oriented governance of projects	SOG1	0,78	0,60	0,25
		SOG2	0,69	0,48	0,23
		SOG3	0,85	0,72	0,28
		SOG4	0,72	0,52	0,23
		SOG5	0,86	0,75	0,28
Project Success	Project efficiency	PE1	0,79	0,62	0,20
		PE2	0,68	0,47	0,17
		PE3	0,63	0,39	0,16
		PE4	0,73	0,53	0,18
		PE5	0,75	0,56	0,19
		PE6	0,47	0,22	0,12
		PE7	0,76	0,58	0,19
		PE8	0,78	0,61	0,20
	Organizational benefits	OB1	0,69	0,48	0,25
		OB2	0,70	0,49	0,25
		OB3	0,69	0,48	0,25
		OB4	0,83	0,68	0,30
		OB5	0,82	0,67	0,29
	Project impact	PI1	0,81	0,66	0,27
		PI2	0,89	0,80	0,29
		PI3	0,91	0,82	0,30
		PI4	0,88	0,77	0,29
	Future potential	FP1	0,65	0,43	0,28
		FP2	0,75	0,56	0,32
		FP3	0,81	0,65	0,34
		FP4	0,86	0,74	0,36
	Stakeholder satisfaction	SS1	0,78	0,61	0,28
		SS2	0,86	0,73	0,31
		SS3	0,86	0,74	0,31
		SS4	0,84	0,71	0,30

Second order construct	First order construct	Item	L[1]	Com.[2]	Weight
Stakeholder Salience	Power	PO1	0,77	0,59	0,40
		PO2	0,86	0,74	0,45
		PO3	0,77	0,59	0,40
	Urgency	UR1	0,85	0,72	0,37
		UR2	0,85	0,73	0,38
		UR3	0,90	0,82	0,40
	Legitimacy	LE1	0,89	0,80	0,51
		LE2	0,43	0,18	0,24
		LE3	0,89	0,79	0,50

[1]*Loadings.*
[2]*Communalities.*

Table 2.
Measurement model.

Second order construct	First order construct	Items	AVE[1]	C.A.[2]	C.R.[3]	KMO[4]	Dim.[5]
Project Governance	Stakeholder-oriented governance of projects	5	0,61	0,84	0,83	0,83	1
Project Success	Project efficiency	8	0,50	0,85	0,84	0,86	1
	Organizational benefits	5	0,56	0,80	0,80	0,71	1
	Project impact	4	0,76	0,89	0,88	0,83	1
	Future potential	4	0,59	0,77	0,79	0,71	1
	Stakeholder satisfaction	4	0,70	0,85	0,84	0,82	1
Stakeholder Salience	Power	3	0,64	0,71	0,76	0,64	1
	Urgency	3	0,75	0,84	0,84	0,70	1
	Legitimacy	3	0,59	0,60	0,74	0,53	1

[1]*Average variance extracted.*
[2]*Cronbach alpha.*
[3]*Composite reliability.*
[4]*Sample adequacy.*
[5]*Dimensionality.*

Table 3.
Validation of the measurement model.

- All constructs presented convergent validation (stroke >0.40).
- All constructs presented Cronbach's Alpha (CA) or Composite Reliability (CR) above 0.60. That is, they all showed the required levels of reliability.
- In all constructs the Factorial Analysis adjustment was adequate, since all KMOs were greater than or equal to 0.50.
- All the constructs were unidimensional by the criterion of parallel lines.

4.3 Factorial analysis of the second order construct stakeholder salience

Table 4 presents the factorial analysis of the Stakeholder Salience construct. Thus, items with a factor load of less than 0.50 should be removed from the analysis because, by not contributing in a relevant way to the formation of the latent variable, they undermine the scope of the basic assumptions for validity and quality of the indicators created to represent the concept of interest. However, all items had a factorial load higher than 0.50.

4.4 Validity, reliability, and dimensionality

Table 5 shows the validity and quality measures of the Stakeholder Salience construct. Thus, we have that:

- All constructs presented convergent validation (stroke >0.40).
- All constructs presented Cronbach's Alpha (CA) or Composite Reliability (CR) above 0.60. That is, they all showed the required levels of reliability.
- In all constructs the Factorial Analysis adjustment was adequate, since all KMOs were greater than or equal to 0.50.
- All the constructs were unidimensional by the criterion of parallel lines.

4.5 Moderating effect

Table 6 shows the direct and moderating effect. Thus, it is possible to conclude that:

Second order construct	Item	L[1]	Com.[2]	Weight
Stakeholder salience	Power	0,61	0,38	0,37
	Urgency	0,80	0,64	0,48
	Legitimacy	0,80	0,65	0,48

[1]*Loadings.*
[2]*Communalities.*

Table 4.
Measurement model of the stakeholder salience.

Second Order Construct	Items	AVE[1]	C.A.[2]	C.R.[3]	KMO[4]	Dim.[5]
Stakeholder Salience	3	0,56	0,60	0,71	0,60	1

[1]*Average Variance Extracted.*
[2]*Cronbach Alpha.*
[3]*Composite Reliability.*
[4]*Sample adequacy.*
[5]*Dimensionality.*

Table 5.
Validation of the measurement model of the stakeholder salience.

Models	Variables	PE		OB		PI		FP		SS	
		β	P-value	β	P-value	β	P-value	β	P-value	β	P-value
Direct effect of stakeholder-oriented governance on project success variables	**SOG**	0,13	**0,023**	0,08	0,094	0,04	0,506	0,12	**0,030**	0,08	0,139
Moderating effect of stakeholder salience	SOG	0,27	0,336	0,27	0,287	0,09	0,776	0,39	0,166	0,08	0,767
	SS	0,41	0,084	0,42	0,053	0,33	0,196	0,52	0,029	0,34	0,156
	SOG*SS	−0,04	0,569	−0,05	0,424	−0,02	0,839	−0,07	0,305	0,00	0,954
Moderating effect of power	SOG	0,35	0,268	−0,02	0,955	−0,02	0,959	0,15	0,648	0,17	0,594
	PO	0,21	0,381	−0,01	0,950	−0,01	0,982	0,01	0,968	0,17	0,483
	SOG*PO	−0,05	0,474	0,03	0,717	0,01	0,862	−0,01	0,936	−0,02	0,791
Moderating effect of urgency	SOG	0,01	0,949	0,15	0,397	0,08	0,704	0,32	0,089	−0,04	0,843
	UR	0,06	0,710	0,25	0,077	0,24	0,161	0,41	0,009	0,14	0,392
	SOG*UR	0,03	0,563	−0,02	0,678	−0,01	0,819	−0,06	0,247	0,03	0,539
Moderating effect of legitimacy	SOG	0,27	0,212	0,19	0,334	−0,07	0,762	0,12	0,587	0,01	0,961
	LE	0,37	0,035	0,24	0,147	0,11	0,571	0,19	0,302	0,15	0,412
	SOG*LE	−0,04	0,408	−0,03	0,512	0,02	0,702	−0,01	0,923	0,01	0,823

Table 6.
Direct and moderating effect for the total database.

There was significant influence (p-value = 0.023) of stakeholder-oriented governance on project efficiency. With each unit that stakeholder-oriented governance increases, project efficiency also increases by 0.13 units.

There was significant influence (p-value = 0.030) of stakeholder-oriented governance on future potential. With each unit that stakeholder-oriented governance increases, future potential also increases by 0.12 units.

There was no moderating effect of the Stakeholder salience construct or even any of its three elements (power, urgency, and legitimacy) on the relationship between stakeholder-oriented governance and each of the five project success items (project effectiveness, organizational benefits, project impact, future potential, and stakeholder satisfaction).

5. Discussion and conclusion

When analyzing the moderating effect of stakeholder salience on the relationship between stakeholder-oriented governance and project success, the authors first verified the existence and the strength of a direct relationship between stakeholder-oriented governance and the five elements of project success. It was possible to conclude that, when Stakeholder Salience is not moderating the relationship between stakeholder-oriented governance and each element of project success, the indicators Project Efficiency and Future Potential are highlighted. These specific indicators were significantly affected, demonstrating that the relationship with them not only exists, but is stronger. Hence, it is possible to conclude that with each unit increase in stakeholder-oriented governance practices, project efficiency will also increase by 0.13 units and future potential, 0.12 units.

Secondly, the authors used the general construct of stakeholder salience and each of its elements (power, legitimacy, and urgency) as moderators to the relationship between stakeholder-oriented governance and each element of project success (Project Efficiency, Organizational Benefits, Project Impact, Future Potential, and Stakeholder Satisfaction), but there was no impact identified on this relationship. This result is different from what was hypothesized by this study's authors. Limited resources make it impossible for managers to care equally about all stakeholders, so Trevino and Weaver [24] stated that those perceived as more salient should receive more attention. Still, the authors concluded that under the Brazilian context, different than what was hypothesized, stakeholder salience, or even any of its elements, did not influence the relationship between stakeholder-oriented governance and each element of project success. This suggests that if a project team desires to improve the performance of these specific success indicators through the implementation of more stakeholder-oriented governance practices, it is not the stakeholders' salience that will serve as a catalyst to this relationship. Hence, it is not a stakeholder characteristic that the project team should be concerned with or put effort on controlling, for it will not affect these indicators.

There are certain limitations as the sample covered was comprised exclusively of Brazilian projects and stakeholders. Research on the cross-cultural impact of stakeholder salience is, therefore, encouraged. This demographic characteristic of the sample could carry cultural bias affecting the results. The same study should be conducted in various countries and cultures before theoretical generalization can be made.

Considering the study's focus on the Brazilian context, it is pertinent to consider the potential for enriched findings through comparative analysis with other cultural or organizational contexts. Previous research indicates that cultural differences can significantly influence stakeholder salience and governance practices. For example, in more collectivist societies, stakeholder engagement and the perception of salience might be more deeply influenced by community and relational values compared to individualist cultures where autonomy and direct stakeholder benefits may predominate [25, 26]. Additionally, organizational practices in different sectors and cultural backgrounds may reveal varied prioritizations of stakeholder groups, suggesting that the framework of stakeholder-oriented governance could benefit from adaptations to reflect these diverse settings [27]. Therefore, a comparative approach could uncover nuanced understandings of stakeholder salience's role in project success across different cultural landscapes, offering broader applicability and deeper insights into the dynamics of stakeholder-oriented governance.

The finding that stakeholder salience does not serve as a moderating variable in the relationship between governance practices and project success in the Brazilian context prompts further reflection. One possible explanation for this observation could be the unique characteristics of organizational culture and stakeholder dynamics within Brazilian companies. In Brazil, the strong emphasis on personal relationships and network-building could mean that the informal practices of stakeholder engagement play a more significant role than do formal governance structures in determining project success. This cultural specificity might dilute the expected moderating effect of stakeholder salience as defined in more formalized or institutional contexts.

Furthermore, preliminary considerations suggest that alternative moderating variables, such as organizational culture, project complexity, and the nature of stakeholder engagement, could provide valuable insights. For instance, the degree of project complexity might interact with governance practices in a way that affects project success differently, depending on the stakeholders' expectations and the project's scope. Similarly, the nature of stakeholder engagement—ranging from consultation to active participation—might influence the project's success outcomes in various industries. These factors hint at a complex web of influences where stakeholder-oriented governance practices are but one component.

To partially address these considerations, our study begins to explore the impact of organizational culture on governance effectiveness. Preliminary analysis suggests that in organizations with a culture that highly values stakeholder input and collaboration, governance practices are more closely aligned with project success, irrespective of stakeholder salience. However, this observation warrants further empirical investigation to understand the conditions under which different moderating variables come into play.

Furthermore, different stakeholders may have different perceptions of stakeholder salience and its elements, so the perception of other stakeholders should also be considered for future research. Stakeholders' theory perceives the relationship between management and stakeholder groups as one of the most vital functions of the organization [26]. In this regard, managers who work to balance the needs of various stakeholder groups are likely to achieve improved organizational performance [28–30]. As already stated, limited resources make it impossible for managers to care equally about all stakeholders, so Trevino and Weaver [24] stated that those perceived as more salient should receive more attention. Other authors stated that perhaps stakeholders should be given equal treatment since researchers have noted stakeholder theory suggests that management uses the homogeneity approach among stakeholders [26, 30, 31]. Another alternative is that salience, in Brazil, should be measured using other core assumptions, i.e. equity, since Schwartz and Carroll [32] declared that stakeholder theory emphasizes the importance for managers to consider equity as an important factor when assessing competing stakeholder needs. Equity, and these other factors, may be considered better moderators for the relationship and should be further studied, for these are all opportunities for future research.

Conflict of interest

The authors declare no conflict of interest.

Author details

Marcela Castro[1*], Paula Misan Klajnberg[2] and Andre Baptista Barcaui[3]

1 Instituto Politécnico de Setúbal, Escola Superior de Ciências Empresariais (ESCE), Setúbal, Portugal

2 Rennes School of Business, Rennes, France

3 Universidade Federeal do Rio de Janeiro, Faculdade de Administração e Ciências Contábeis (FACC), Rio de Janeiro, Brazil

*Address all correspondence to: marcela.castro@esce.ips.pt

References

[1] Rowley T. Moving beyond dyadic ties: A network theory of stakeholder influences. Academy of Management Review. 1997;**22**(4):887-910

[2] Cohen J. Stakeholder engagement: A key driver for project success. Project Management Journal. 2021;**52**(3):258-272

[3] Frooman J. Stakeholder influence strategies. Academy of Management Review. 1999;**24**(2):191-205

[4] Breman E, Trott P. Strategic management of stakeholders: Theory and practice. Long Range Planning. 1999;**32**(3):330-340

[5] Jones R et al. Strategic stakeholder management in project environments. Journal of Project Management. 2022;**40**(1):45-62

[6] Smith A, Brown L. Prioritizing stakeholder engagement in project management. International Journal of Project Management. 2023;**41**(2):286-299

[7] Wang S et al. Stakeholder salience and project success: A moderated mediation model. Journal of Business Ethics. 2021;**175**(3):611-626

[8] Lee H, Kim M. Understanding stakeholder power dynamics in project governance. Project Management Journal. 2023;**54**(1):35-50

[9] Wang X, Chen Y. Quantitative research on project governance and success in the IT industry. Journal of Project Management. 2006;**15**(3):45-62

[10] Müller R, Martinsuo M. Relational norms in project networks: A case study. International Journal of Project Management. 2015;**33**(3):650-662

[11] Joslin R, Müller R. Relationships between a project management methodology and project success in different cultural contexts: An empirical investigation. Project Management Journal. 2014;**45**(6):30-44

[12] Smith A et al. Stakeholder salience in governance strategies: A comprehensive analysis. Journal of Business Ethics. 2021;**89**(4):567-583

[13] Jones P, Brown C. Dynamic stakeholder relationships in project governance. Project Management Journal. 2023;**54**(2):198-214

[14] Mitchell RK et al. Toward a theory of stakeholder identification and salience: Defining the principle of who and what really counts. Academy of Management Review. 1997;**22**(4):853-886

[15] Boaventura JMG. Stakeholder theory: A Brazilian perspective. International Journal of Management and Business Research. 2012;**2**(2):143-159

[16] Parent M, Deephouse DL. A case study of stakeholder identification and prioritization by managers. Journal of Business Ethics. 2007;**75**(1):1-23

[17] Johnson EA et al. Power dynamics in project environments: An empirical investigation. Project Management Journal. 2021;**52**(4):389-404

[18] Zhao X, Wei L. Navigating power dynamics: Stakeholder engagement in project management. International Journal of Project Management. 2023;**41**(2):275-288

[19] Mintzberg H. Power in and around Organizations. NJ, EUA: Prentice-Hall; 1983

[20] Liu Y et al. Resource allocation and project success: The role of power dynamics. Project Management Journal. 2020;**51**(6):647-662

[21] Mitchell RK, Agle BR. Legitimacy and power in stakeholder relationships. Journal of Business Ethics. 2022;**171**(2):321-336

[22] Miles S. Legitimacy and the chain of command: Communication, perception, and influence. Journal of Applied Psychology. 2002;**87**(4):542-553

[23] Brown AD, Dillard JF. Stakeholder legitimacy and decision-making: An exploration of the concept and its application. Journal of Business Ethics. 2023;**172**(1):105-121

[24] Trevino LK, Weaver GR. The stakeholder research tradition: Converging theorists - not convergent theory. Academy of Management Review. 1999;**24**(2):222-227

[25] Hofstede G. Culture's Consequences: International Differences in Work-Related Values. Beverly Hills, CA: Sage Publications; 1980

[26] Freeman R. Strategic Management: A Stakeholder Approach. London: Pitman; 1984

[27] Jones TM, Wicks AC, Freeman RE. Stakeholder theory: The state of the art. In: Crane A, McWilliams A, Matten D, Moon J, Siegel DS, editors. The Oxford Handbook of Corporate Social Responsibility. Oxford: Oxford University Press; 2002. pp. 17-47

[28] Gibson K. The moral basis of stakeholder theory. Journal of Business Ethics. 2000;**26**(3):245-257

[29] Laplume AO, Sonpar K, Litz RA. Stakeholder theory: Reviewing a theory that moves us. Journal of Management. 2008;**34**(6):1152-1189

[30] Verbecke A, Tung V. The future of stakeholder management theory: A temporal perspective. Journal of Business Ethics. 2013;**112**:529-543

[31] Neville BA, Bell SJ, Whitwell GJ. Stakeholder salience revisited: Refining, redefining, and refueling an underdeveloped conceptual tool. Journal of Business Ethics. 2011;**102**:357-378

[32] Schwartz MS, Carroll AB. C. Corporal social responsibility: A three domain approach. Business Ethics. 2008;**13**:1-22

Chapter 5

Perspective Chapter: The Principles of Corporate Governance are an Advantage or a Necessity to Promote the Transparency of the Capital Market

Mohammad Hormozi

Abstract

Corporate governance is defined as a set of rules and principles governing the correct management of a company, in order to manage it, to control the conflict of interests or to eliminate it as much as possible, and to use the company's assets to maximize the interests of investors. Corporate governance can be considered as a control process that exists between managers, shareholders and stakeholders to ensure the interests of all owners and stakeholders, a process that has control in the direction of accountability, more transparency in providing information and proper reporting. Corporate governance is one of the common concepts in today's business world, which has been raised since the 1990s in the industrialized countries of the world. In Iran, since 2003, measures have been taken by the stock exchange organization to establish corporate governance. It is obvious that in order to attract investors to the country's capital market, which leads to economic growth, the implementation of the principles of corporate governance should become a mandatory process, so that the risk of investors is reduced, and for this reason, their confidence to invest in the capital market and finally to improve transparency in the market. Let's be capital.

Keywords: corporate governance, accountability, conflict of interest, capital market, economic growth and development

1. Introduction

The capital market as one of the financial organs of the country's economy has a special place and can take effective steps to improve the economic growth and development of the country. Something that exists all over the world, and productive economic sectors benefit from it, and they fund capital through this market, and they take their development plans and they continue to live, and sometimes they go from small workshops and medium-sized companies to large, multidisciplinary companies, and they export their products to all countries of the world. So, the more you can strengthen the capital market in the country, the more you can hope for the growth and development of different sectors, and most importantly, important economic infrastructure and infrastructure. The role of corporate governance principles and their proper implementation by the members of the board of directors of companies as representatives of investors and the supervisory role of the Securities and Exchange Commission as a reference and legislative body will be more prominent in this sector because one of the important factors in attracting the maximum amount of large and small capital and small savings is that many people in the community who can become a very large national capital in total create trust for them to have the maximum benefits by reducing the risk of investing they are going to continue to invest and we are going to see capital outflows. We are not going to be on the stock market. The capital that we have seen in previous years was imported into the coin or dollar sector, causing chaos and chaos in the country's economy, and not helping the country's economy grow and develop.

2. Corporate governance is an important factor for capital market transparency

In this article, we are looking for an answer to the question of whether to increase the transparency of information and the satisfaction of shareholders and other stakeholders to invest in the country's capital market should the implementation of corporate governance principles in joint stock companies be considered an advantage or should an executive and committed necessity be considered for company managers?

2.1 The importance of the subject

Iran has a lot of investment opportunities, investments that are often made by the private sector and domestic companies, and sectors that are waiting for foreign investors and suppliers to enter; if domestic companies are well supported or can attract capital through the capital market, they can complete half-finished projects and advance their new plans for the economic growth and development of the country, such as many foreign companies. So, the importance of this is that the unity of society with all its capital and savings should contribute to this growth and development, and one of these ways is the capital market, which by properly implementing and enforcing the principles of corporate governance we can gain the trust of large and small investors, and by accumulating these assets, we can expect more progress in different sectors of the economy.

2.2 Research method

The main objective of this research is to examine the necessity of implementing the principles of corporate governance as a commitment in companies to increase the confidence of investors in different sectors of society in the capital market; therefore, it is placed in the category of Applied Research and its method is analytical and inferential, and also in the compilation of this article, library resources and the study of domestic and foreign books and articles and authoritative sites have been used.

2.3 Theoretical concepts and research background

2.3.1 Corporate governance

Corporate governance, as defined by the organization for economic cooperation and development (OECD), is the procedures and processes by which the organization is guided and controlled. The corporate governance structure distributes the rights and responsibilities of the various activists of the organization such as the board of directors, directors, shareholders, and other stakeholders, to determine the events and procedures for decision-making [1].

2.3.2 Responsiveness

When the principles of corporate governance are properly implemented in joint-stock companies, whenever any of the shareholders, investors and beneficiaries need information about the company, they will receive the right answer at the right time. Accountability will be accompanied by transparency in such a way as to express the real economic situation of the company as it is. This means that the company informs the shareholders of the information in the information conferences, including the contracts and the implementation of important and influential projects, or creates groups in social networks so that this information reaches the awareness of all the shareholders, or through the shareholder portal. Every company. In general, companies have created special communication ways to respond to their shareholders [2].

2.3.3 Conflict of interest

This means that the person in charge is between personal and nonpersonal interests (others such as shareholders and other stakeholders). As mentioned, corporate governance implements structures and processes in the company through which all the responsibilities and duties of the board of directors, CEOs, and shareholders can be properly divided, interpreted, and explained so that we see a systematic regulatory system, including the audit committee, the salary and benefits committee (compensation of services), and the appointment committee so that all matters are controlled by the members of these specialized committees to ensure the performance of managers with shareholders, and in this case, the length of the division of control tasks will become more responsive and transparent, and the conflict of interest will create healthy and stable relationships in companies [3].

2.3.4 Capital market

The capital market is one of the most important economic elements in the country, which is referred to as the thermometer of the economy. The financial market for buying and selling securities or bonds with maturities of more than one year and assets without maturities is called the capital market. In the most common division, the capital market is divided into two primary and secondary markets in terms of the supply stage of securities, and in another division in terms of the conditions of companies, they are classified into two stock markets and over-the-counter. There is another subset of the stock market and the stock market, each of which has specific terms and conditions; and companies will be accepted in these markets according to the conditions they have at the time of admission to the stock market or the stock market. The capital market is like a bridge that transfers small and large community savings to companies in need of capital, thus directing this useless capital to produce and create more value so that we can finally see the economic growth and development of the country, and on the other hand, investors not only gain from this shareholding but also feel satisfied with the contribution to the growth and maturity of their country. Another function of the capital market is to fund the government's finances. When governments face a shortage of resources, they borrow from the people through the supply of bonds in a way that they can implement current affairs or construction projects and similar things at the macro and national levels.

2.3.5 Economic growth and development

Economic growth is the increase in a country's production in a particular year compared to its value in the base year, and in the macro dimension, the increase in gross national product (GNP) or GDP in the year under review is considered economic growth compared to its value in a base year. The reason why the base year prices are used to calculate economic growth is that the calculated increase in GDP is due to the increase in production and the impact of the increase in prices (inflation) is eliminated. If national production increases in a country, it can be said that there is economic growth in that country. Economic development is economic growth combined with fundamental changes in the economy and increasing production capacities so that it can find new markets to sell its products or compete with other countries.

As we know, corporate boards are among the most important mechanisms of corporate governance and play a prominent role, managers who, with different roles in the specialized committees of joint stock companies, formulate and manage the company's policies and guide the organization with proper supervision and methodology.

Fama and Genesis [4] believe that the board plays a pivotal role in corporate governance as it is considered one of the main pillars of corporate governance in today's world and is often referred to as the executive lever of corporate governance principles and responsible for policy-making and control in companies.

Klein's [5] studies also show that larger boards have more effective management oversight, and that the effectiveness of boards is related to the composition of boards (in terms of duty and non-duty) in addition to its size.

Chen and Jaggi [6] have made their arguments about the importance of nonboard members. First, they say that nonexecutive directors make the company's board announcements available to others regarding strategic decisions. Second, non-employee managers are more motivated to control and monitor the decisions, programs, and activities of the company's executives. They see the board of directors, with a majority of nonexecutive directors, as more responsible and responsible than shareholders 'demands for transparency and disclosure and tend to improve the breadth and quality of disclosure of the company's information, which will result in a reduction in the lack of information intervention between internal and external individuals.

Sarhangi and Jalali Farahani [7] conclude in a study titled the impact of ownership structure on the profit sustainability of companies admitted to the Tehran Stock Exchange that ownership structure has a significant impact on profit sustainability, as well as a significant relationship between institutional ownership, larger shareholder ownership and profit sustainability.

In his study titled "examination of the relationship between institutional ownership and profit information content", gholamreza Karmi [8] tested the relationship between institutional ownership and profit information content and concluded that institutional ownership does not promote the company's profit information content and may reduce it.

Jamshidi Navid and Izadi [9] in a research titled the study of the impact of applying the principles of corporate governance on the behavior of investors in the Tehran Stock Exchange, stated that companies as the economic pillar of the society in creating wealth and employment and attracting capital are known. Observance of shareholders' rights, transparency of information, and fulfillment of social responsibilities by companies are among the most important factors that have been paid more attention than in the past. The corporate governance law is a set of relationships between shareholders, managers, auditors of the company, which includes the establishment of a control system in order to respect the rights of shareholders, except for the correct implementation of the resolutions of the assembly, as well as to prevent abuses. It is possible. This law, which is based on the accountability and social responsibility system, includes a set of duties and responsibilities that must be carried out by the company's elements to ensure accountability and transparency.

2.3.6 Findings

Currently, the member states of the organization for economic cooperation and development consider the principles of corporate governance as a measure of the performance of their companies. Principles and policies that should be codified beyond the economic, political, cultural, and social situations of countries and implemented with the supervision of reference institutions and organizations. For example, in Iran, the Securities and Exchange Commission and the reference organization are responsible for this; in order to strengthen the confidence of investors in the country's capital market by establishing specific regulations and statutes in the field of corporate governance, we must prevent the entry of incompetent managers at the levels of the board of directors of companies to witness the correct and correct implementation of the principles of corporate governance in the management of companies, which seems more important and necessary in the capital market of the country, so that we can see more transparency, no misleading shareholders, and no secret misuse of information by managers. What will attract more investor satisfaction and lead to the boom and growth of the country's capital market? We will describe the objectives of these principles and the characteristics of an effective corporate governance system.

2.3.7 Principles of corporate governance

1. Provide a legal basis for the formation of the corporate governance framework (through the drafting and adoption of appropriate laws and monitoring its proper implementation)

2. Preserving the rights of shareholders and the main functions of ownership (through the establishment of a proper legal system.)

3. Fair treatment of shareholders (respect for the rights of minority shareholders and the authorization of minority supervision of the company's activities.)

4. Respect for the rights of all stakeholders (through transparent and timely reporting of information)

5. Disclosure and transparency (through appropriate regulatory laws and increased enforcement guarantees of laws and regulations.)

6. Definition of responsibilities of shareholders, boards, CEOs, and development of supervision and controls, including internal control devices, internal audit, and independent audit (**Figure 1**) [10].

These defined principles for a good corporate governance should be considered by investors and by analyzing these principles, they should correctly identify the stocks of the top companies in the capital market, because companies that are bound and committed to the implementation of these principles are an order of magnitude less investment risk than companies that do not. They either do not implement the principles correctly or ignore them at all, and they mostly pursue their personal interests in companies to pursue the interests of shareholders and other investors. In companies where these principles are implemented correctly, in the first step, the partial shareholders have a special position and the major shareholders alone will not be the main decision makers of the company. When appropriate laws are established for the formation of good governance, company managers at different levels always know that all the actions and decisions they take will be monitored by other supervisory managers through a series of laws, and in this way, they avoid inappropriate and contrary actions to these laws. The interests of investors and shareholders were not jeopardized. In the following, each of these six principles is explained, the importance of corporate governance is stated, and the structure of this system is outlined.

The first of these principles is the formation of the corporate governance framework. (1) The corporate governance framework should increase the transparency and efficiency of the capital market, be in accordance with laws and regulations, and clearly divide responsibilities among regulatory units, legislation, and authorized

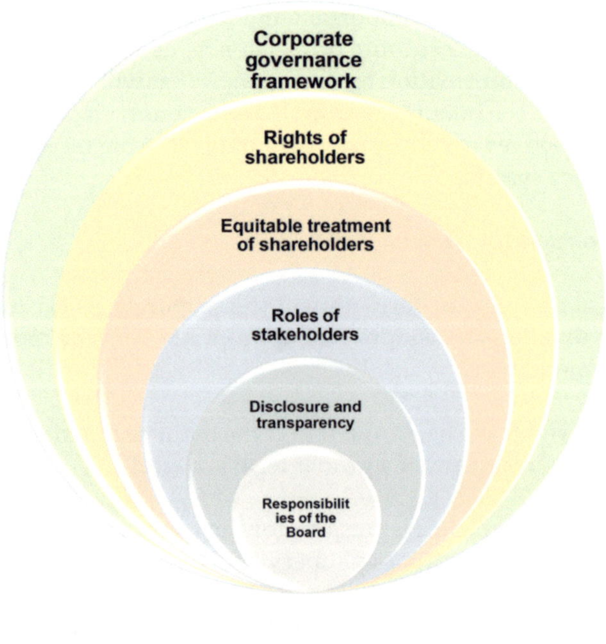

Figure 1.
Principles of corporate governance-Organization for Economic Cooperation and Development (OECD).

persons. (2) The corporate governance framework should protect the rights of shareholders and facilitate its application by shareholders. (3) The corporate governance framework should ensure fair treatment of shareholders including minority and outsourced shareholders. All shareholders should be given the opportunity to receive their damages from those who have lost their rights. (4) The corporate governance framework shall respect the rights of the beneficiaries established by law or bilateral agreements. (5) The corporate governance framework shall ensure that important matters regarding the financial status, performance, ownership, and governance of the company are properly and continuously disclosed.

The second principle of corporate governance is the protection of shareholder rights, and for this, there are criteria that, if observed, increase the trust of shareholders in investing in the company. Here, it is better to have a definition of shareholder rights, and rights arising from ownership of shares are numerous and are mentioned in various articles of the commercial law. In general, these rights are divided into two categories: financial and nonfinancial rights, financial rights arising from the ownership of shares: the right to share in profit, the right to advance in the new shares of the company (in order to preserve the rights and position of the shareholder in the company), and the right to share in the company's assets. Nonfinancial rights: including voting rights and the right to notice.

1. Voting rights: The shareholder participates in the company's affairs such as the election of the members of the board of directors and the company's inspectors, capital changes, profit sharing, statute changes, company dissolution, and other matters, using his voting rights in public assemblies. Right of transfer of shares: the shareholder can transfer his shares to another person at any time by referring to the broker by it.

2. Right of notice: The right of shareholders to know the status of the company is a means of proper exercise of the right to vote. Each shareholder can go to the accounts 15 days before the general meeting at the company center and receive a transcript of the financial statements from the balance sheet.

It is clear that when the principles of corporate governance are properly implemented in a company, these rights are respected, shareholders feel more satisfied, their trust and opinion are attracted, and they manage their capital and do not leave the company. For example, one of these is the payment of interest approved by the corporate assemblies, which according to Article 240 of the commercial law of joint stock companies, are obliged to pay the annual interest approved to shareholders within eight months after the decision of the ordinary general assembly companies that delay in paying interest is considered to be legally violators but are not punished and in fact paying interest is a legal duty which if not respected is punishable by a fine that is not paid. However, in most countries of the world, the profits approved by the assemblies are immediately paid to shareholders and if companies do not comply with their legal duties' shareholders can sue companies and claim their rights and rights a mechanism that we have not yet implemented in our country. In some developed countries of the world, the profits approved by the assembly are paid to shareholders within five days, and this means the correct and correct implementation of the principles of corporate governance; something that we in our country, unfortunately, do not take seriously and professionally and do not consider as a major policy and policy for the capital market of the country. The issue that most shareholders they complain about it, and they see delays in paying their profits as a waste of their rights, and they see it as one of the regulatory weaknesses of the reference organizations.

The third principle of corporate governance is the fair treatment of shareholders, or in other words, the respect for the rights of minority shareholders and the authorization of minority supervision of the company's activities, one of which is the increase in the capital of companies, which is still approved in corporate assemblies, a bill that is certainly very decisive for major shareholders to achieve and will implement their opinions. This is the point where shareholder rights are not considered part of when companies only increase capital to get out of their financial problems, not increase shareholder wealth, so that if shareholders are very unhappy with this trend because they believe that their capital has been lost in most of these capital increases because after the capital increases and the number of shares increases, the sales pressure is created, and eventually with the increase in supply over demand, the stock price will fall and shareholders will suffer losses, which means the loss of shareholder rights and the loss of shareholders 'rights their distrust of the country's capital market, an issue that has been discussed in numerous scientific, and the university of the country has been recognized and pathologized.

The fourth principle of corporate governance refers to the observance of the rights of all stakeholders through transparent and timely reporting of information, for example, companies where major shareholders have extensive control over all matters of the company, and apply their opinions also have important and key information that only circulates in a particular circle, and shareholders are often unaware of them, so they can become less aware of the company's operations, the level of transparency of information will be very low and therefore the possibility of misuse of the company's financial resources will increase. Information in the general sense includes knowledge or a group of knowledge that forces a person to change his or her position and make a decision or revise a decision when necessary. Information is today the most valuable and key possession in the capital market so that the gains and losses incurred from the investment depend on whether or not this information is true or false in the market, something that we are witnessing in the stock market at the moment, rumors that sometimes occur in relation to different companies in the market are that a car company has signed a contract with a European partner or a European partner. Even selling shares to them to sell an island to a company to do their project or even news of a thousand percent capital increase from the place of accumulated profit and revaluation of assets of a company that is not transparent and is not properly informed or even denied by the managers of companies and creates a scam, and as a result, these shareholders are part of the company that suffers great losses [11].

The presence of sufficient information in the market and the rapid and timely reflection of information on the price of securities means market efficiency, and the economic goals expected from the capital market are mainly achieved in market operating conditions. In the market, the information that is distributed in the market quickly affects the price, and in such a market, the price of securities approaches its intrinsic value. in other words, the important feature of the market is that the price set in the market is a good indicator of the actual value of the securities. In such a market, the price of securities, such as the price of ordinary shares, reflects all the information available in the market, and thus the level of public trust that meets the requirements and the institutional background of quantitative development in the dimensions of value increase, volume, and number of transactions, and it is strengthened. The most important factors in theory are useful information and accuracy, timeliness, citability, and inferability. Given the breadth of the scope of the information discussion, we realize that capitalized companies are only part of the elements that affect this relationship [12].

The fifth principle of corporate governance is disclosure and transparency through appropriate regulatory laws and increased enforcement guarantees of laws and regulations so that the appropriate information of the companies is accurately and timely in relation to all related issues, including the overall performance of the company, financial situation, and ownership structure, and in other words, is better accountable to the request of the shareholders. The internal nature of the company's disclosure tends to increase the transparency of the company's financial and operational performance by providing useful information so that internal and external users, the majority of whom are shareholders, benefit from it in their business and economic decisions. Financial reporting standards significantly emphasize the needs of external users. Financial statement information helps shareholders assess the company's past performance, ability, weaknesses, liquidity, debt repayment ability, and management effectiveness. Financial statements also help shareholders evaluate cash flows that affect the intrinsic value of shares. In order for financial information to be clear and transparent, it should not be misleadingly presented. Readers of financial statements should be able to understand financial statements without additional effort. To achieve this, annual financial statements must include full disclosure and a greater amount of transparency [13].

The sixth principle of corporate governance is to define the responsibilities of shareholders, boards, and CEOs and develop supervision and controls, including internal control devices, internal audits, and independent audits. Strategic plans and guidelines for effective supervision of directors by the board of directors, and how the board of directors responds to the company and shareholders are identified. The secret of a company's success lies in its desirable guidance, so it can be claimed that the secret of the immortality of famous and well-known companies is their effectiveness in the effective and efficient board of directors. The board of directors of the company is considered its heart, so it must always be healthy, cheerful, and well-fed. Board meetings should be held regularly and as planned, and in the board, it should not be allowed for a particular person to master the board meetings and the decision-making process and impose their opinions on others. There is a balance of power between the board members so that no one is able to "unconditionally" control the decision-making process within the company. In addition, the division of responsibilities at the highest level of the company must be clearly defined to ensure the balance of power and the limits of the powers of the board members. The Hampel report (1998) reviewed the duties and roles of nonexecutive directors but did not propose an increase in their desired number on the board. On the other hand, the desired composition of the proposed members of the board of Directors (nonexecutive) in the comprehensive law (1998) has not changed from the number recommended in the Cadbury law. In both laws, it is emphasized that the number of nonexecutive directors (nonexecutive) should not be less than one-third of the number of board members.

2.3.8 The importance of corporate governance

1. The process of privatization and market-based investment is one of the most important economic issues of the day. Privatization has increased the amount of corporate governance in the sectors that have been previously held by the government and companies are forced to resort to the market to provide capital, so they have tried to be admitted to the stock exchange.

2. Due to technological advances, trade liberalization and other structural reforms, especially in the field of deregulation of the pricing sector and removal of ownership restrictions, the way capital is allocated among national and supranational companies has undergone its own complexities.

3. The movement of capital from personal ownership to corporate ownership has increased, and the role of financial intermediaries has increased in other words; the role of institutional investors has become more prominent in many countries.

4. Reform programs in the field of financial issues have reshaped this part of the domestic and foreign economies of countries.

5. Increased financial cohesion at the international level and investment and transaction turnover have led to issues in the field of international issues.

2.3.9 Corporate governance goal

The ultimate goal of corporate governance is to achieve fairness, transparency, accountability, and respect for the rights of stakeholders in the economic enterprise. The financial performance of companies is directly related to the exercise of their corporate governance rights, and better managers make corporate governance more effective, pay attention to their stakeholders and ultimately generate more financial returns. Among the expectations of managers are the ability to generate growth, timely repayment of commitments, creating value for shareholders, Working group, risk management and control, communicating with the environment, and advancing goals [14].

2.3.10 Corporate governance structure

Intraorganizational corporate governance (German–Japanese) is a system in which the listed companies of a country are under the ownership and control of a small number of major shareholders. These shareholders may be the founder or a small group of shareholders such as creditor banks, other companies, or the government. Intraorganizational governance mechanisms (surroundings) include board of directors, executive directors, nonexecutive directors, internal control and organizational ethics.

Outsourced corporate governance (Anglo-American) refers to financing and corporate governance systems in which large companies are controlled by managers and are owned by outsourced shareholders or private shareholders. This situation leads to the separation of ownership from control. External (environmental) governance mechanisms include legal supervision, legal regime (establishment of appropriate legal system), capital market efficiency, supervision of major shareholders (motivation of shareholders to activities such as purchasing), role of institutional shareholders (encouragement and expansion of institutional investors), supervision of minority shareholders, and mandatory independent auditing [15].

2.3.11 Components of the internal corporate governance structure

1. Simple balance sheet model indicates the basis of the representation relationship. It includes the internal mechanisms of corporate governance. As a representative of the owners, the management decides on the selection of the appropriate assets (projects) for investment and how to finance the resources needed. The board

of directors is also responsible for advising management and monitoring how it operates, as well as installing, removing, and determining the remuneration of high-level managers [16]. On the other side is the structure of the company's external capital, which comes from the company's financing needs. This separation has led to the demand for the use of corporate governance structures.

2. The framework model of the board of directors: The internal corporate governance structure is divided into five groups: (1) The board (their position, structure, and motives), (2) The motives of the executive directors, (3) The provisions of the statute and statutes (such as the means of dealing with the ownership bills), (4) The capital structure, and (5) The internal control systems of the company.

The factors of the external governance structure of the company can also be divided into four Groups: (1) Type One markets, including capital markets, corporate control market, labor market, and product market, (2) Type two markets, which emphasize the preparation of capital market information (such as capital market analysts, debt and corporate governance structure), (3) Type three markets, which focus on accounting, financial, and legal services provided by individuals and consultants outside the company, they emphasize, and include auditing, liability insurance for company managers and consulting with investment and investment banks, and (4) Laws and regulations [17].

2.3.12 Accountability

Accountability is a set of social relationships that a person feels committed to explaining and justifying their behavior and relationships with others. Here, we can divide accountability into two parts. First: To make clear and explicit the information that applies to the general shareholders. Second: Officials and managers who consume resources should be accountable to shareholders about how to manage these resources and express their reports clearly. The most important accountability tool is the company's financial reporting management, which discloses the information required by stakeholders. The leaked information must-have features to meet the needs of users. The most important feature of this leaked information is transparency so that it can be relied on. In companies where these principles are implemented correctly, we see that shareholders have expressed a high percentage of their satisfaction with the way managers operate, and this will increase the growth and growth of the country's capital market.

3. Conclusion

Shareholders and investors in the stock exchanges are important components of the country's capital market those who promote the market by entering their small and large capital, and accumulating; this capital can raise the financial problems of many small and large companies and not only help the growth and development of the country but also keep the investor satisfied by increasing wealth and profitability; but all of this value chain in the group is a good and desirable governance a decent and knowledgeable management that is guided by a high policy, which is the same as the principles of corporate governance and by implementing the right principle to gain shareholder trust in such a way that the risk of investors is as high as possible. As long as they see that they have good investment opportunities in our country and that the accepted international standards and corporate governance principles are properly implemented, they are encouraged to do this investment, and the result is nothing but the development of the capital market and the development of the economy. The importance and place of implementing corporate governance principles in large and developed countries are well understood, and it is important to remind us that corporate governance principles are more of a commitment to shareholders and investors than an executive advantage, and we also need to develop a commitment to shareholders and investors. We have no way to implement the legal and disciplinary framework for the correct implementation of these principles.

Achievements of corporate governance in Iran

In the country of Iran, about two decades ago, very important and effective measures were taken in line with the implementation of corporate governance and correct management of companies, exactly when the Ministry of Economy and Finance, the Central Bank and the Stock Exchange and Securities Organization of Iran decided with collective wisdom. Anti-money laundering laws and regulations, as well as the principles of corporate governance, follow the implementation of these regulations seriously, and based on this, useful guidelines for companies, especially companies listed on the stock exchange, were prepared and set up and communicated to all companies. Currently, we see that good progress has been made, companies take utmost care in appointing board members and try to choose suitable and competent people who have knowledge and skills related to the field of work of that company and maximize efficiency and profitability for the company. The company earns to be the criterion of action. This is a very important thing achieved through corporate governance. Among the other things that can be mentioned is that in Iran, after two decades, the reporting of companies has changed, and the transparency of information about listed companies has become very desirable so that companies are obliged to provide quarterly, six-monthly audited interim financial information, and nine-monthly and yearly audits and also to disclose all the information related to conducting transactions and entering into important contracts. To do this, a website has been designed under the name of www.codal.ir, which allows all investors and beneficiaries of the Iranian capital market to check the financial status of companies, do the necessary research, and refer to this website. The important point is that the Iranian Stock Exchange Organization has considered certain punishments and crimes for companies that do not fulfill their duties within the legal deadlines and do not disclose their information in a timely and complete manner, and the managers of the companies in order to deal with this problem from the side of the stock exchange organization do not be confronted, and they mainly send their companies' information to be published in the Codal system by the specified deadline. Disciplining companies and disclosing financial information is one of the most important achievements of corporate governance in Iran. Today, we all know that if large and active companies in a country do their work with information and financial transparency without any organized corruption; this will spread to other economic sectors of the country such as banks, customs, offices, and organizations, and this is nothing but growth. It will not bring economic development to the country precisely when all the economic components of a country work together to help each other and facilitate each other's work like interconnected gears. When domestic and foreign investors are faced with the transparency of financial statements and financial discipline of companies and can find a suitable and safe place for their capital, it is obvious that they have the incentive to invest and buy shares of companies, the potential that currently exists in Iranian companies. Undoubtedly, the entry of new investment and the injection of money into companies will lead to their growth and development, which is usually recorded in numerous practical articles with econometric models and its results, and we are all aware of the positive results of the entry of capital from foreign investors. It will affect the economy of countries and will cause their growth and development. Certainly, one of the other important achievements of correct and principled corporate governance is the persuasion and encouragement of foreign investors so that they can plan on the profitability of other companies in addition to their business plans and investment models that currently manage their assets. In Iran, many plans have been made to further encourage foreign investors, if we want to mention only one of them, it is the issue of tax exemption for foreign investors, as well as the permits that they need to obtain a stock exchange code and open a bank account in Iran will be issued as soon as possible.

If we want to mention another achievement of corporate governance in Iran, we can mention the structuring of companies and the regulatory role of corporate governance for all people working in the company and a clear hierarchy, just where in corporate governance, the need to create specialized committees of the board of directors is mentioned. This makes the levels of an organization clear, the deputy and senior managers know their duties correctly and refer all the affairs and works to their subordinates accordingly, and in this way, we are faced with an organization and company with disciplined and orderly administrative procedures in such a way that every employee, the expert, manager, senior manager, managing director, and board of directors know the description of the duties of doing their work correctly, and this prevents wasting time, and thus improves the productivity of the organization. This is another achievement of corporate governance.

Another achievement of corporate governance is risk management in companies. Whether companies are active in the public sector or in the private sector, it is very important that companies use their resources where the best results can be achieved. At first glance, what is imagined for capital market analysts is that the amount of financial resources wastage is high in government companies, and in these types of companies, due to the connection with the government and the deposit of government funds to them, and the funds that these companies have through the communication between government organizations have and sometimes the lack of careful monitoring on the selection of plans and projects leads to financial resources being wasted, and in private companies, risk management is carried out in a way by the type of shareholders who are also mainly owners so that they can get the most productivity and profit with the least amount of risk. Iran, such as other countries, is an important issue regarding state-owned companies. In these two decades, corporate governance has been able to systematize the structure of state-owned companies to a great extent with its guidelines, and the result has been very tangible in Iran, as is evident in auditors' reports and financial statements of companies and economic statistics published by reliable institutions in Iran. Corporate governance has stated very important issues to the members of the board of directors of companies in the direction of risk management, one of the most important of which is to respect the rights of shareholders, and the members of the board of directors of companies are representatives of companies who must perform their duties properly and protect the interests of their shareholders and take care and wherever they feel that the interests of the shareholders are in danger, they should not accept the risk, and they should be extremely careful in carrying out affairs and choosing plans and projects. All these things that were mentioned above are among the most important achievements of the correct implementation of the principles of corporate governance in Iran, each of which has been the source of positive effects in the direction of the growth of companies and the development of corporate knowledge.

4. Proposal

As supreme councils are formed to monitor the proper implementation of a series of laws and regulations or to amend and approve a set of statutes and guidelines in different parts of the country, for example, the supreme council for combating money laundering or the higher council for education operating in its specialized areas, it is proposed that the supreme council for corporate governance be formed at the level of the Ministry of Economic Affairs and Finance or the Securities and Exchange Commission to approve regulations and binding statutes for companies admitted to the stock exchange and the faraborus witnessed the formation of a new stage in the path of growth and let us be the progress of the country's capital market. The council may, by law, perform the following duties: It has:

1. Collect and obtain relevant and up-to-date information and news, principles of corporate governance and social responsibility, and analyze and classify them technically and professionally.

2. Summarize and standardize new issues raised in the field of corporate governance in the world to apply them within the country.

3. Preparation and proposal of the necessary regulations on the correct and correct implementation to the supreme council of the country's stock exchange or the board of directors of the stock exchange and securities organization

4. Integrate the relevant organizations and coordinate with each other in pursuing the full implementation of the decisions of this council.

Thanks

Thanks to my hero father who is always alive in my heart.

Also, my loving mother, my beloved wife, and my beautiful daughters, Yalda and Yasna, who have always been my friends and companions in my life.

Author details

Mohammad Hormozi
Head of Corporate Affairs Department of Atiyeh Andishan Mes Investment Company, Iran

*Address all correspondence to: mhormozi11@gmail.com

References

[1] OECD Guidelines on Corporate Governance of State-Owned Enterprises. Available from: www.OECD.org

[2] Kose J, Senbet LW. Corporate governance and board effectiveness. Journal of banking. Finance. 1998;**20**:371-403

[3] Freeman ER. The politics of stakeholder theory: Some future directions. Business Ethics Quarterly. 1994;**4**:409-421

[4] Fama EF, Jensen MC. Separation of ownership and control. Journal of Law and Economics. 1983;**16**:301-325

[5] Klein A. Audit committee, board of director characteristics, and earnings management. Journal of Accounting and Economics. 2002;**33**:375-400

[6] Chen CJP, Jaggi B. Association between independent nonexecutive directors, family control and financial disclosures in Hong Kong. Journal of Accounting and Public Policy. 2000;**19**:285-310

[7] Sarhangi H, JalaliFarahani Abas. The Impact of Ownership Structure on the Sustainability of Profits of Companies Admitted to the Tehran Stock Exchange, Accounting and Auditing Research Quarterly; 2014. No:24. The code of conduct of the company, adopted in 2007 by the Tehran Stock Exchange

[8] Karmi G. Investigating the relationship between institutional ownership and the informational content of profits. Tehran University Accounting and Auditing Reviews. 2007;**54**:81-100

[9] JamshidiNavid B, Izadi MM. Examination of the impact of the use of corporate governance on the behavior of investors on the Tehran stock exchange. Journal of Financial Engineering and Securities Management. 2011

[10] OECD Principles of Corporate Governance. Paris: OECD; 2004. Available from: www.Oecd.org/dataoecd/31557724/18/32.pdf

[11] Baber WR, Kang SH, Liang L, Boards S. Management Entrenchment and Accounting Restatement, Working Paper,. Washington, DC: George Washington University; 2005

[12] Islami G. Information of the most important asset in the stock market. Fund. 2005;**64**:5

[13] Mousavi R, Jabari H, TalebBidokhti A. Corporate Governance and Renewal of Financial Statements, Financial Accounting and Auditing Research Quarterly; 2015. No:25

[14] Chiang H. An empirical study of corporate governance and corporate performance. Journal of American Academy of Business. 2005;**6**:95-101

[15] Gillan SL, Starks L. Corporate governance, corporate ownership, and the role of institutional investors: A global perspective, journal of applied. Finance. 2003

[16] Jensen MC, Meckling WH. Theory of the firm: Managerial behavior, agency costs and ownership structure. Journal of Financial Economics. 1976;**3**(4):305-360. DOI: 10.1016/0304-405X(76)90026-X

[17] Norosh I, Karmi G, Vafi Thani J. Investigating the relationship between the mechanisms of the company's management system and the agency costs of the companies admitted to the Tehran stock exchange. Accounting and Auditing Research (Accounting Research). 2009;**1**:4-27. Available from: https://sid.ir/paper/157309/fa

Chapter 6

Perspective Chapter: Governing Corporations in Appearance but Not in Fact – A Possible Unintended Consequence of the Corporate Governance Movement

Khalid Al-Adeem

Abstract

Corporate failures trigger corporate regulations. The corporation is a fiction that is theorized as a nexus of contracts. Mechanisms for monitoring corporations, namely the external audit function and corporate governance, have been promoted and propagated. Whether corporations are governable is a question. An argument made in the accounting literature is that the audit function has been successful because of the ability of external auditors to appear independent when they might not be. The board of directors of such corporations may appear governing executive managers while they are in fact not or cannot. With the ideology of "profit over people," multinational companies run the world with CEOs who are the most powerful individuals in the corporate model. Without corporate financers' active involvement, corporations are unleashed. Corporate financers need to be aware of their power and be able to hold executive management accountable to make their corporations good citizens of the globe. Corporate monitoring mechanisms do not make up for their absence in the corporate model, which makes the view that corporations are founded to maximize the value of absentees naïve. A long history of corporate failures has proven its fallacy.

Keywords: corporate model, corporate accounting, monitoring, external auditing, corporate governance

1. Introduction

Corporate failures trigger corporate regulations. The scandal of the Kreuger Corporation in the 1930s that the US capital market experienced during the Great Recession, though contributed to the US financial reporting [1], has not stopped corporate failures and scandals. By providing information about the corporation before the public offering, the Securities Act issued in 1933 safeguarded the US capital market from applying Ivar Kreuger's strategy. The Security Act of 1934 mandates the continuation of disclosing corporate financial data annually; establishing an agency to oversight corporate reporting and watchdog corporations in the US.

The Sarbanes–Oxley Act (SOX) in 2002 was issued as a quick governmental response to the scandals of Arthur Andersen's clients, namely Enron and WorldCom. Governments worldwide, for example, Saudi Arabia, issued a bulletin to govern corporations in 2006 after the Saudi capital markets experienced a downfall in 2006. The bulletin is updated in 2009, 2015, 2017, 2018, and 2023. Patching the bulletin shall continue because governing corporations is not constructed on a sound theory of the firm nor does corporate governance stand as a sound theory. In fact, neither has the corporate model been fully comprehended nor has the corporate accounting function been completely understood. The concern is that the best that can be achieved is a corporation that *appears governed while in fact is not*. This outcome is not new to the corporate model. To maintain the corporate model, the external auditor appears independent [2] because being independent in fact is no longer professionally required nor can he be independent.

Following the issuance of corporate regulations that took place at the beginning of the current millennium, a wave of corporate governance has spread almost worldwide. Recently corporate governance has been propagated as a mechanism that is capable of monitoring corporations. Corporate governance become in some of the world as a profession to a wide range of individuals. Corporate governance models have been proposed to assist in monitoring executive management of corporations.

This chapter is for the public to shed light on the complex nature of corporations and the impossibility of governing them. Multinational corporations that rule the world [3] are not subject to initiatives of being governed. The conjecture is that corporate governance can be in place in appearance but in fact. Such a proposition calls to hypothesize that a certain type of individual fits to become the board of directors. Probably individuals who are serious about governing corporations may not be able to fill seats on the board of directors of some corporations. The corporate model has not been fully understood nor adequately theorized [4].

The remainder of the chapter is organized as follows. The following section highlights our understanding of the corporation. Section 3 brings to attention the challenge that the corporate model represents. Section 4 is about the lasting issue that resulted from the separation between management and ownership. Section 5 addresses the possibility that with the absence of corporate financers corporate governance can be achieved only in appearance. Section 6 concludes that corporations are on unleash unless their financers become aware and actively involved. If they cannot, then the corporate model is needed for an appropriate, probably realistic, theorization and the role of corporate accounting should be expanded.

2. What is corporation?

The firm, as the literature reveals - see, for example, the law literature - is a fiction, [5] that does not have a physical existence. Its existence is juridical or legal [6]. The argument in the law profession (e.g. [7–15]), in economics [16, 17] about what the corporation has not yet been settled to date. Such divergent views were extended to the accounting literature as well [4, 14, 18, 19].

Viewing the corporation as a "nexus of contracts" prevails and seems to dominate other views in the economic and law literature. The promoters of the contemporary stream of accounting research seem to adopt such a concept as well [20–28][1]. The variety of arrays of relationships that encompass the corporation form an enterprise where each party has a stake in it. Greenwood [74], however, argued that stakeholder participation in running a corporation possibly would overlap with the moral behavior of stakeholders; nevertheless, it may "run counter to moral" conduct.

The enterprise theory views the firm as a reporting accounting entity to a variety of stakeholders [75–77]. The enterprise theory in accounting institutes corporate reporting that serves all stakeholders' interests [78].

The "nexus of contracts" view necessitates monitoring the corporate reporting function that promotes the external audit function. Recently, major corporate scandals have called for activating corporate governance mechanisms suggested decades ago. Corporate governance goes back to 1932 [79][2]. These two mechanisms are challenges associated with the c corporate model.

3. The corporation: a model for conducting business representing a challenge

Since its emergence, the corporation has represented an accounting challenge. Early accounting pioneers recognized the challenge. Littleton [80].

> *"Moderns have produced these business corporation with its far-flung ownership and its limited liability to place upon accounting burdens of which the ancients did not dream. For example, objections to dividends out of capital are of recent origin, and because of these objections much added importance is now attached to properly determined periodic profits. These are sources for much of modern theory.*
>
> *Business is now regarded as a continuous process rather than a group of disjointed transactions. This is expressed by our development of the terms "earnings" and "income" in contrast with "profits"."*

Measuring corporate performance is probably one of the most puzzling tasks that accounting confronted to date. Previts and Merino [81] articulate, "[a]ccountants responded creatively and effectively to... [the separation of ownership and control] challenge...accounting theorists had developed a historic cost allocation model that effectively silenced questions about the relevance of accounting profit and reaffirmed the primarily of ownership rights." However, the inherently random techniques associated with cost allocation are a drawback that impairs the wished-for results of allocation techniques and brings troublesome disputes [82–84][3]. Former SEC Chief Accountant Walter Schuetze said: "Allocation is used for managing earnings to smooth the hills and valleys of change."

Defining income and profit is one of longest debating unsettled concepts in accounting [80, 86–108].

[1] Probably positive accounting research that Watts and Zimmerman promoted is the most criticized methodology in the accounting literature [29–72]. This does not disqualify Professor Watts from being admired for promoting what he believes [73].

[2] NA: The date of publication is unknown. The manuscript is in the Arabic language.

[3] Wiring in 1978, Zimmerman [85] claimed that the cost allocation concept existed in the accounting profession and literature for over 75 years.

In addition, the divergent interests of the parties who make up the corporation differ and occasionally conflict. Innovations have been proposed to align controverting interests. For example, generous corporate executives' compensation plans have not been an effective means for encouraging corporate executives to serve the interests of corporate financers, mainly shareholders.

External auditing as a corporate monitoring mechanism has not been an effective device in the corporate model [2, 63, 90, 93, 109–136]. Due to the challenges in acquiring contact with real-life information, inquiry virtually into auditor-client relationships is conjectural or ancillary ([137], as cited in ([138], p. 13) and Dye 1991, as cited in ([138], p. 13). Theoretically, the corporate model permits collaboration between any two parties that might not be in the best interest of other parties [123]. Professional corporate managers may behave improperly against the interests of investors and shareholders [139]. Auditors are incentivized to collaborate with executive managers to form a partnership that might not be in the best interest of shareholders [140]. Interviewed executive managers and auditors reported that the auditor might be powerless to defend third parties from management fraud [141].

The corporate scandals, to be exact Enron and WorldCom, that occurred at the beginning of the current millennium called for governmental actions to restore confidence in the corporate model. Arthur Anderson, who once symbolized the culture of values in the auditing market, audited the two failed corporations. The failure of external audits fuelled the aggressiveness of the US government. A republican government signed SOX in 2002. Similarly, governments worldwide, for example, Saudi Arabia, issued a bulletin in 2006 governing corporations in their lands after capital markets experienced a downfall in Ref. [142] and keep updating it [143–147] to articulate and state corporate responsibilities toward the public.

Conventionally unlike the democratic type of government, republicans are promoters of market solutions that are constructed on not interfering with market mechanisms. The market shock, however, was beyond any plan for containing. The market shock required a response with a magnificent scale. Corporate governance, which is so long inactive component of the corporate model, was reactivated with a full scale.

The roles of the board of directors and audit committees have been emphasized. Members of such boards and committees ought to actively participate in the governing activities of their corporations. However, the existence of corporate governance does not guarantee governing executive management in a way that assures alignment with their interest and parties financing the corporation. The ability of the audit committee is doubted [148]. KPMG (2004 as cited in ([149], p. 242)) reported, "Even though Sarbanes-Oxley significantly increased the role of the audit committee, client management remains most influential with regard to issues such as auditor retention and compensation." Empirical exploration shows that the board of directors is not an effective mechanism for governing executives in Saudi Arabia [150].

Whether corporations are governable is a question. The issue for society and stakeholders is when a corporation can appear as a governed entity while in fact, it is not. This issue is not new to accounting. The concept of auditor in appearance has been divided into two sub-concepts: independent in appearance and independent in fact [109], an indicator of the impossibility of maintaining independence in truth. Independence is a state of mind. "[O]nly the auditor himself or herself knows for sure whether...[independence in fact] has been compromised" [151].

4. The separation between management and ownership: the lasting issue in corporate economy

The separation between management and ownership [152] brought into existence a challenge facing accounting of how to report to external parties about corporate internal affairs that affect the financial position of the reporting entity [2, 4, 32–34, 81, 87, 140, 153–155].

Given the fact that the corporation is the result of cooperative contracted parties each of which is serving his/her interest, the conflicting interests among such parties permit theorizing the corporations as an agency issue. Jensen and Meckling [156] observed "...agency costs arise in any situation involving cooperative effort... by two or more...." Fogarty et al. [157] deemed Jensen and Meckling [156] a "rediscovery." The agency issue is not new to accounting. Agency as a model for theorizing the corporation was rediscover but not invented to assist in mitigating risk that the corporate model for conducting business brings to stakeholders of the incorporated enterprise. [158, 159]. Agency relationship in Italy was an important concept because it forced accountability; the concept was later important to the development of corporations [159]. With risky equity particularly with respect to the action of agents, such risks were offset by the deep personal loyalties of covenants deriving from kinship bonds" ([158], p. 52).

Agency theory is a dogma [160] that has dominated accounting research worldwide (e.g. [29, 33, 54, 71, 161–173]) to the extent it has dictated the accounting publishing market in the US to become an immutable theoretical foundation in top-tier accounting outlets [30, 174, 175].

The agency model that is used for theorizing corporations is incomplete. The principal in the agency relationship is actually absent [2, 154, 155, 176]. Stockholders tend to invest in corporations through intermediaries [177]. When individual investors incorporate shares, they tend to hold them for short periods that can last seconds [178]. Individual investors do not appear as investors who make decisions regarding their investments [177, 179, 180]. Institutional investors are the main corporate investors.

Modeling the corporation as an agency requires encompassing the agency between shareholders and mutual funds that manage the investment of shareholders [181]. The agency model is then two-tier: the first tier is between executive management and mutual funds managers while the second is between mutual fund managers and shareholders [181].

In comparison to other parties in the corporate model, the chief executive officer (CEO) is the most powerful individual. Defiant investors are weak in comparison to the executive management of their corporation [180, 182]. Empowering shareholders is yet another myth [183] which is the myth of shareholder maximization value myth [184–197][4]. Mutual funds directors who are supposed to be the agents of shareholders in the contractual relationship between executive management and shareholders do not participate in governing corporations [180].

The audit function, as a conventional mechanism for safeguarding the shareholders' interest, as well as corporate governance, the current mechanism of newly enacted regulations reactivated, might not be as effective as hoped [109, 140, 187].

---

[4] For more on the discourse in this book, an issue of *Accounting, economics, and law: A convivium* was dedicated to a review of the book in addition to other reviews, for example, Schrempf-Stirling [198].

Executive management prefers a close relationship with their auditors [2, 109, 199]. Empirical confirmation reveals the client's first choice for a relational tactic with their auditors ([200], p. 4). External auditors cannot always resist the demands of the executive management whose financial statements they are auditing [109]. Executive management has numerous prospects to conspire in hiding transactions from the auditor ([201], p. 121). Executive management employs financial accounting standards in ways best serve their interest [23]. Bost [118] contended "...auditing firms too often lost their independence and become overly accommodating to their clients in deferring to questionable accounting stratagems." In some circumstances, external auditors find it optimal to cooperate with the executive management [140]. Chung & Kallapur [202] conjectured that auditors' motivations to compromise their independence are associated with client status.

Strengthening auditor independence has not been successful in a corporate setting [109, 140, 201]. The Securities and Exchange Commission (SEC) keeps providing details for circumstances where auditor independence might be breached (e.g. [201]) an indicator of the impossibility of performing corporate auditing with total impartiality [114–116, 129, 140]. Because of lacking independence, auditors are perceived as synonymous with 'CEO,' and 'CEO' does not stand for anything good ([203], p. 30), is identified with the client "in the public eye" ([204], p. 34), and create "long-term cooperative partnerships with their clients"[5] (Max Bazerman). The same can arguably happen to the corporate governance mechanism in a corporate setting [111].

A board of directors might not be powerful in comparison to executives as it is propagated [199, 205]. Board of directors do tasks that in nature are extensions of the tasks assigned to executive management [180]. The SOX narrowed directors' focus on financial reporting risk at the expense of strategy and introduced some variation in the extent and nature of the role performed by the audit committee to decide accounting differences of opinions and to give thought to varying construal of law [206]. If corporate executives' compensations signify their value, then a marginal role is left for the board of directors [199].

A board of directors as a monitoring corporate mechanism is not newly added to the corporate model. Their role has been recently reemphasized after major corporate failures at the beginning of the current millennium. Without a board of directors' actual involvement in monitoring corporate executives, the risks and consequences of corporate executives' decisions are overnighted.

5. Corporate governance in appearance: A possibility

5.1 The prescribed remedy is not curing

Since the corporation is viewed as an agency, the risk of making decisions that may affect the wealth of owning parties who do not participate in managing their enterprises can be arguably controlled through monitoring mechanisms [207]. The Sarbanes–Oxley Act (SOX) was the major piece of legislation since the Great Depression [208]. Brown Jr. [208] described it as dilapidated bills, with very diverse philosophies, that were cobblestoned, amplified, and passed in an outbreak of action. Drawn it up in haste [209] does not make the SOX a perfect remedy.

---

5 Max Bazerman, Creating Auditor Independence. Availed online: http://pcaobus.org/Rules/Rulemaking/Docket037/ps_Bazerman.pdf Last visited June 28, 2015.

The SOX was a prompt governmental response to restore confidence in the capital market. Reviews of studies on the impact of the SOX suggest that investors' confidence was assured [210, 211]. Anandarajan et al. [201] however asserted the claim that while "investors may have been lulled into feeling comfortable about audit firm performance given the clear legal penalties that the audit firms face...This...is an area for future research that has not been thoroughly examined." While others might still deem the movement toward effective corporate governance revolution and attribute it to the SOX [212–214], it is best described as a wave.

SOX's effect in comparison to the cost of its implementation is questionable [215]. Some perceive its costs exceed its benefits [216] while others argue that it is not sufficient for the enhancement of corporate governance [217]. It has not necessarily discouraged actual fraudulent behavior [218].

It is a phenomenon that corporate scandals create a demand for regulating corporations. The Securities Act of 1933 and 1934 followed the great depression. SOX followed the failure of two major Arthur Anderson's audit clients, namely Enron and WorldCom. A quick governmental response does not cure the capital market from its norms nor does it yield the hoped outcomes.

5.2 The complexity of governing corporations

Listing six myths surrounding corporate governance; Brickley & Zimmerman [219] concluded that understanding the nature of corporate governance is not a one-person task. The issue that Berle and Means [152] raised must be understood for any monitoring mechanism to be workable. While an independent board of directors is a convention, evidence suggests that an independent board of directors is correlated with worse corporate performance [220].

With the ideology of "profit over people" [221], multinational companies run the world [3], affecting strategically their affairs for example the consumption of citizens of a variety of countries [222]. Similarly, societies change because of participating in capital markets. The US has become an equity culture [223] and has grown into an "ownership society" [184] that has instigated a public change in the US. In seeking liberty and equality as an alternative to relying on their government, such public has become investors instead of savers [224].

Accounting and auditing are myths and rhetoric [132, 225–228]. Accounting reality is constructed [229, 230] but not a reflection of the economic reality underlying the enterprise [231]. Accounting truth has been always a challenge [225, 232–235]. Recently a discourse has emerged as a result of FASB's approach of constructing reality [236–242] which is added to the debate on accounting truth and reality [225, 229, 232–235, 243–253]. Professor Sterling's [256] warnings [257] and others' warnings of the coming crisis in accounting [258] have been ignored. While playing their number game [259], accountants are unaccountable [260] and auditors are unaudited [261, 262]. In response to a Fortune writer regarding the story that the Wall Street Journal ran in 1994 in a front-page story detailing the many ways that Jack Welch and his team smoothed earnings at General Electric (GE), a GE staff member indicated that the people at GE received calls from other corporations (AIG, Champion International, and Cigna) and commented that "Well, this is what companies do. Why is this a front-page story?" [263]. The current accounting system permits such activities [264].

Moreover, the analysis of several proposed models that Jensen & Meckling [265] analyzed reveals the superiority of the Resourceful, Evaluative, and Maximizing Model (REMM). The REMM suggests that if a person finds an opportunity to benefit, he intends to exploit it and benefit from it, and the same applies to him if he is placed under pressure. Arguably, an individual may respond to it, especially if the return from responding to these pressures is greater than adhering to the position dictated by his work requirements. If there are incentives that compensate for the cost or consequences of responding to these more beneficial pressures, then it is economically optimal to comply with these pressures. Management executives, accountants, external auditors, and the board of directors apply to them what applies to humans [266]. Auditors economically represent their self-interest [267]. Financial statements fraud as a form of corruption is a systematic activity [268] that cannot be in place with the organization to deviations from norms [266] and without personnel carrying out such activities [269].

Two years after enacting SOX, Mitchell [214] concluded:

> *"One could dare hope for the eventual development of a new investment culture in which stockholders buy and hold for the long-term, investigating their companies and reading financial information and other disclosures before investing. One can hope. Whether the regulations are vigorously enforced, or whether the SEC is lax, whether institutional investors continue to exert short-term pressure on management, and whether the market's recent need for instant gratification continues, remain to be seen."*

Twenty years later, one would argue the corporate economy has experienced its norm where fraud behavior deceived individual investors.

Mimicking theory suggests that an enterprise can mimic another to signal to the market that the former is as good as the latter. A corporation may theoretically employ a corporate governance mechanism to signal that its executive management is governed. The board of directors of such corporations may *appear* governing executive managers while they are *in fact* not or cannot. The audit function has been successful arguably because of the ability of external auditors to *appear* independent while *in fact* they might not be independent [2].

Government regulations alone are not sufficient to establish financial markets that nurture auditor independence ([270], p. 269) as well as effective and true corporate governance. Humans are complex creations. Without a code of values, they tend to rationalize what best serves their interest. Unless the code of values has control over humans' actions in the corporation, any proposed remedy does not guarantee a cure. If this is too much to ask, then the corporate model needs to be revisited.

6. Conclusion

The old slogan, 'fake it until you make it' fits the continuing efforts in minoring the risk brought as a result of founding enterprises that are led and managed by those who did finance them. Corporations can only appear as they are wished to appear, but unlikely to be in fact as wished.

'Guard it before you lose it' is better to become an action plan and put in place for corporate financers. Involvements of all stakeholders might not yield effective and efficient corporate governance [74]. Oppositions to shareholder power are myths [187].

Awareness of corporate financers is what is needed. Without their active involvement, corporations are unleashed. When they become aware and realize that they may not be able to hold executive management accountable to make their corporation a good citizen of the globe, they can react and make decisions. Inordinate shareholder power is correlated with superior corporate performance in all deliberate matters [187].

Once becoming aware, the public's reaction to corporations is magnificent. The best example of exercising the public power would be the blockage that the public undertakes to join Palestine's suffering and pain caused by the invading people who are supported by powerful international countries affected international corporations. Starbucks bled because of its stand on oppression and injustice to innocent people in Palestine. The government of South Africa has brought a case against the oppression of people in Plantain in the International Court. None of these have happened in the past decades. Palestine had been in the past the case of Arabs and Muslims. Things changed, as the public became aware of reality with a clear vision and without illusion.

Furthermore, the emerging need for the utility of ethics in accounting due to an unsettled environment in which accounting operates and the changes in science call for normative accounting theorization where ethics underline it philosophically, epistemologically, and methodologically [271]. Operationalizing "the accounting function...to serve information needs within a particular cultural environment and... reflect related social, economic, political, and legal influences" ([272], p. 137) potentially assists corporate accounting in serving the public. Accounting has been responding to societies' economic needs [4, 32–34, 75, 111, 112, 140, 153, 154, 273–288]; Montgomery as cited in Nelson [289]) and shall continue once the corporate model is theorized soundly and realistically. The view that corporations are founded to maximize the value of absentees is naïve. A long history of corporate failure has proven its fallacy.

Future research can explore the types of individuals, who are suitable to serve as members of a corporate governor in appearance. Illiterate individuals whose knowledge in accounting, finance, and business is weak and individuals who are willing to cooperate with the executives probably fit such types of people.

Acknowledgements

I am indebted to Case Western Reserve University for granting me access to the resources through the KSL Alumni Online Library, which made completing this article possible.

Author details

Khalid Al-Adeem
Professor of Accounting, College of Business Administration, King Saud University, Saudi Arabia

*Address all correspondence to: kra3case@gmail.com; kaladeem@ksu.edu.sa; khalidaladeem@gmail.com

References

[1] Flesher DL, Flesher TK. Ivar Kreuger's contribution to US financial reporting. The Accounting Review. 1986;**61**(3):421-434

[2] Al-Adeem KR. Revisiting the role of accounting from ancient to contemporary times: An attempt to evaluate the role of corporate accounting. Strategies in Accounting and Management. 2022b;**3**(4):1-13

[3] Korten DC. When Corporations Rule the World. 2nd ed. Boulder, Co.: Kumarian Press; 2001

[4] Al-Adeem KR. A need for theorizing corporation: An accounting perspective. International Journal of Accounting Research. 2017a;**5**(2):166

[5] Jalal MB. Principles of Economics. Riyadh, Saudi Arabia: Alanwar Publishing House; 1965 [In Arabic]

[6] Al-Adeemm KR. Accounting Information System: Objectives, Concepts and Applications. Saudi Arabia: Amotanabe Publishing House; 2019 (In Arabic)

[7] Davis JP. The nature of corporations. Political Science Quarterly. 1897;**12**(2):273-294

[8] Demsetz H. The theory of the firm revisited. Journal of Law, Economics, & Organization. 1988;**4**(1):141-161

[9] Eisenberg MA. The conception that the corporation is a nexus of contracts, and the dual nature of the firm. Journal of Corporation Law. 1998;**24**:819

[10] Hayden GM, Bodie MT. The Uncorporation and the Unraveling of" nexus of contracts" theory. 09 Michigan Law Review. 2011;**1127**:1127

[11] Huber WD. Corporate Law and the Theory of the Firm: Reconstructing Corporations, Shareholders, Directors, Owners, and Investors. Abingdon, Oxfordshire: Routledge; 2020a

[12] Huber WD. Economics, Capitalism, and Corporations: Contradictions of Corporate Law, Economics, and the Theory of the Firm. Abingdon, Oxfordshire: Routledge; 2020b

[13] Kornhauser LA. The nexus of contracts approach to corporations: A comment on Easterbrook and Fischel. Columbia Law Review. 1989;**89**(7):1449-1460

[14] Reve T. The firm as a nexus of internal and external contracts. In: The Theory of the Firm: Critical Perspectives on Business and Management. 1990. pp. 310-334

[15] Easterbrook FH, Fischel DR. The Economic Structure of Corporate Law. Harvard University Press; 1996

[16] Lazonick W. Business Organization and the Myth of the Market Economy. Cambridge: Cambridge University Press; 1991

[17] Williamson O. The Economic Institutions of Capitalism. New York: Free Press; 1985

[18] Biondi Y, Canziani A, Kirat T. The Firm as an Entity: Implications for Economics, Accounting and the Law. Abingdon, Oxfordshire: Routledge; 2008

[19] Suojanen WW. Accounting theory and the large corporation. The Accounting Review. 1954;**29**(3):391-398

[20] Watts RL. Corporate financial statements, a product of the market and

political processes. Australian Journal of Management. 1977;**2**(1):53-75

[21] Watts R. The Evolution of Economics-Based Empirical Research in Accounting, The SAXE Lecture in Accounting. 1983. Availabel from: https://academicworks.cuny.edu/cgi/viewcontent.cgi?article=2075&context=bb_pubs [Accessed: August 14, 2023]

[22] Watts RL, Zimmerman JL. Positive accounting theory for the determination of accounting. The Accounting Review. 1978;**53**(1):112-134

[23] Watts RL, Zimmerman JL. The demand for and supply of accounting theories: The market for excuses. The Accounting Review. 1979;**54**(2):273-304

[24] Watts R & Zimmerman JL. The Markets for Independence and Independent Auditors. Working Paper. 1981. Availabel from: file:///C:/Users/User/Downloads/Watts_Zimmerman_MarketsIndp%20(3).pdf [Accessed: November 25, 2020]

[25] Watts R & Zimmerman JL. Auditors and the Determination of Accounting Standards. Working Paper. 1982. Availabel from: file:///C:/Users/User/Downloads/Watts_Zimmerman_Audit&Account.pdf [Accessed: November 25, 2020]

[26] Watts RL, Zimmerman JL. Agency problems, auditing, and the theory of the firm: Some evidence. The Journal of Law and Economics. 1983;**26**(3):613-633

[27] Watts RL, Zimmerman JL. Positive Accounting Theory. New Jersey: Prentice-Hall; 1986

[28] Watts RL, Zimmerman JL. Positive accounting theory: A ten year perspective. The Accounting Review. 1990;**65**(1):131-156

[29] Al-Adeem KR. Role of doctoral education in shaping minds and thinking: Reflection on my doctoral education at Case Western Reserve University. International Journal of Critical Accounting. 2017b;**9**(5-6):494-513

[30] Al-Adeem K. Who decides what is publishable? Empirical study on the influence of a Journal's editorial board on the observed paradigm shift in US academic accounting research. The North American Accounting Studies. 2019b;**2**(1):1-21

[31] Al-Adeem K. Critique and an extension of Nohora García' s understanding Mattessich and Ijiri: A study of accounting thought. International Journal of Accounting and Financial Reporting. 2019c;**9**(4):420-438

[32] Al-Adeem KR. Properly identified imaginary needs, an inaccurately proposed methodology: The case of Rochester school of accountancy's positive accounting methodology. Accounting and Management Information Systems. 2021a;**20**(4):607-645

[33] Al-Adeem K. Empirically investigating the presence of positive accounting research as the meta-theory for accounting academics: Further evidence from Saudi Arabia. The Journal of Accounting and Management. 2021b;**11**(3):26-49

[34] AlAdeem KR, Fogarty TJ. Accounting Theory: A Neglected Topic in Academic Accounting Research. KG: LAP Lambert Academic Publishing AG & Co; 2010

[35] Avelé D. Positive accounting theory: Theoretical and critical perspectives. International Journal of Critical Accounting. 2014;**6**(4):396-415

[36] Belkaoui AR. Accounting, a Multiparadigm Science. Westport, CT: Quorum Books; 1996

[37] Boland LA, Gordon IM. Criticizing positive accounting theory. Contemporary Accounting Research. 1992;**9**(1):142-170

[38] Chabrak N. The politics of transcendence: Hermeneutic phenomenology and accounting policy. Critical Perspectives on Accounting. 2005;**16**(2):701-716

[39] Chabrak N, Burrowes A. The language of the Rochester school: Positive accounting theory deconstructed. In: 8th IPA Conference-the Interdisciplinary Perspectives on Accounting Conference. 2006

[40] Chambers RJ. Positive accounting theory and the PA cult. Abacus. 1993;**29**(1):1-26

[41] Christenson. Methodology of positive accounting. The Accounting Review. 1983;**58**(1):1-22

[42] Collin SOY, Tagesson T, Andersson A, Cato J, Hansson K. Explaining the choice of accounting standards in municipal corporations: Positive accounting theory and institutional theory as competitive or concurrent theories. Critical Perspectives on Accounting. 2009;**20**(2):141-174

[43] Demski JS. Positive accounting theory: A review. Accounting, Organizations and Society. 1988;**13**(6):623-629

[44] Hines RD. Popper's methodology of falsificationism and accounting research. The Accounting Review. 1988a;**63**(4):657-662

[45] Kabalski P. Why should accounting science be more normative? Zeszyty Teoretyczne Rachunkowości. 2016;**88**:61-72

[46] Kabir H. Positive accounting theory and science. Journal of CENTRUM Cathedra. 2010;**3**(2):136-149

[47] Kaplan SE, Ruland RG. Positive theory, rationality and accounting regulation. Critical Perspectives on Accounting. 1991;**2**(4):361-374

[48] Lowe EA, Puxty AG, Laughlin RC. Simple theories for complex processes: Accounting policy and the market for myopia. Journal of Accounting and Public Policy. 1983;**2**(1):19-42

[49] Major MJ. Positivism and "alternative" accounting research. Revista Contabilidade & Finanças. 2017;**28**(74):173-178

[50] Milne MJ. Positive accounting theory, political costs and social disclosure analyses: A critical look. Critical Perspectives on Accounting. 2002;**13**(3):369-395

[51] Mouck T. Irony of the golden age of accounting methodolgy. Accounting Historians Journal. 1989;**16**(2):3

[52] Mouck T. Positive accounting theory as a Lakatosian research programme. Accounting and Business Research. 1990;**21**(79):231-239

[53] Mouck T. The rhetoric of science and the rhetoric of revolt in the "story" of positive accounting theory. Accounting, Auditing & Accountability Journal. 1992;**5**(4):35-56

[54] Ndjetcheu L. An African critical interpretation of the positive theory of accounting of Watts and Zimmerman (1978, 1980, 1986). African Journal of Accounting, Auditing and Finance. 2012;**1**(1):25-39

[55] Okcabol F, Tinker T. The market for positive theory: Deconstructing the theory for excuses. Advances in Public Interest. 1990;**3**:71-95

[56] Persson ME. Foreword. AC Littleton's Final Thoughts on Accounting: A

Collection of Unpublished Essays. Leeds, England: Emerald Group Publishing Limited; 2016

[57] Sinha SK. Positive accounting theory: A critique. The IUP Journal of Accounting Research and Audit Practices. 2008;7(4):7-16

[58] Srivastava J, Baag PK. Positive accounting theory and agency costs: A critical perspective. AIMS International. May. 2020;**14**(2):101-113

[59] Sterling RS. Positive accounting theory: An assessment. Abacus. 1990;**26**(2):97-135

[60] Sy A, Tinker T. Archival research and the lost worlds of accounting. Accounting History. 2005;**10**(1):48-69

[61] Sy A, Tinker T. From Mellmott to Madoff: History in the (re) making. Accounting Historians Journal. 2011;**38**(1):141-158

[62] Tinker T. Panglossian accounting theories: The science of apologising in style. Accounting, Organizations and Society. 1988;**13**(2):165-189

[63] Tinker AM, Merino BD, Neimark MD. The normative origins of positive theories: Ideology and accounting thought. Accounting, Organizations and Society. 1982;7(2):167-200

[64] Tinker T, Puxty T. Policing Accounting Knowledge: The Market for Excuses Affair. Princeton, NY: Markus Weiner Publishers; 1995

[65] West BP. Professionalism and Accounting Rules. New York, NY: Routledge; 2003

[66] Whitley RD. The possibility and utility of positive accounting theory. Accounting, Organizations and Society. 1988;**13**(6):631-645

[67] Williams PF. The logic of positive accounting theory. Accounting, Organizations and Society. 1989;**14**(5/6):455-468

[68] Williams PF. Modern accounting scholarship: The imperative of positive economics science. Accounting Forum. 2003a;**September. 27**(3):251-269

[69] Williams PF. Jumping on the wrong bus: Reflections on a long, strange journey. Critical Perspectives in Accounting. 2017;**49**:76-85

[70] Whittington G. Positive accounting: A review article. Accounting and Business Research. 1987;**17**(68):327-336

[71] Yousof AM. Analyses and critique the foundation of positive theorization in accounting. Business Administration. 2006;**112**:26-35 [in Arabic]

[72] Al-Adeem KR. Book Review of: Understanding Mattessich and Ijiri: A Study of Accounting Thought. European Accounting Association, EAA Newsletter. 2019a. Available from: https://mailchi.mp/f9c88eb16bd9/eaa-newsletter-march-2019-2#Have%20you%20read

[73] Al-Adeem KR. Understanding Professor Ross Watts by applying Kuhnian interpretation of science Progress. Strategies in Accounting and Management. 2023a;**4**(1):SIAM. 000580. DOI: 10.31031/SIAM.2023.04.000580

[74] Greenwood M. Stakeholder engagement: Beyond the myth of corporate responsibility. Journal of Business Ethics. 2007;**74**:315-327

[75] Chatfield M. A History of Accounting Thought. Revised ed. Huntington, New York, USA: R.E. Krieger Pub. Co; 1977

[76] Drucker P. The New Society. New York, NY: Harper and Brothers; 1949

[77] Hendriksen ES. Accounting Theory Revised Edition (November). Homewood, IL: Richard D. Irwin, Inc; 1972

[78] Al-Adeem KR. Accounting as a sustainable crafted technology for human exchange activities with nature: A defense of accounting continuity. Frontiers in Environmental Science. 2023b;**11**:1165247. DOI: 10.3389/fenvs.2023.1165247

[79] Farraj TA, AlAAdhy SA, Jaber A, Jad Alwaly M, Yaqooub O, Ammarah M. Corporate Governance and Accounting Ethics. Cairo, Egypt: Cairo University; [in Arabic]

[80] Littleton AC. Paciolo and modern accounting. The Accounting Review. 1928;**3**(2):131-140

[81] Previts GJ, Merino BD. A History of Accountancy in the United States: The Cultural Significance of Accounts. Columbus, Oh: Ohio State University Press; 1998

[82] Statement on Accounting Theory and Theory Acceptance (SATTA). American Accounting Association Committee on Concepts and Standards for Externals Financial Reports. Sarasota, FL: American Accounting Association; 1977

[83] Thomas AL. The Allocation Problem in Financial Accounting Theory. Sarasota, FL: American Accounting Association, Studies in Accounting Research) No. 3; 1969

[84] Thomas AL. Useful arbitrary allocations (with a comment on the neutrality of financial accounting reports). The Accounting Review. 1971;**46**(3):472-479

[85] Zimmerman JL. 1978 competitive manuscript award: The costs and benefits of cost allocations. The Accounting Review. 1979;**54**(3):504-521

[86] Alexander SS, Bronfenbrenne M, Fabricant, Solomon, Warburton, Clark, "Five monographs on business income; Income measurement in a dynamic economy; Business income concepts in the light of monetary theory; Business costs and business income under changing price levels; Monetary theory and the price level trend in the future; Case against change in present methods of accounting for exhaustion of business property. Association Sections, Divisions, Boards, Teams. 1950;**71** Available from: https://egrove.olemiss.edu/aicpa_assoc/71

[87] Alharbi AM, Al-Adeem KR. A defense on accounting discretion: An empirical inquiry based on users' awareness. Financial Markets, Institutions and Risks. 2022;**6**(3):26-39. DOI: 10.21272/fmir.6(3).26-39.2022

[88] Bangs RB. The definition and measurement of income. The Accounting Review. 1940;**15**(3):353-371

[89] Bauer J. The concepts of capital and income in the regulation of public utilities. The Accounting Review. 1937;**12**(1):22-29

[90] Chang EC. Business income in accounting and economics. The Accounting Review. 1962;**37**(4):636

[91] Crandell WT. Income and its measurement. The Accounting Review. 1935;**10**(4):380-400

[92] Dickinson AL. Profits of a Corporation: A paper read before the Congress of Accountants, at St. Louis, on September 26, Individual and Corporate Publications; 1904. p. 33. Retrieved: https://egrove.olemiss.edu/acct_corp/33/

[93] Edwards EO, Bell PW. The Theory and Measurement of Business Income. Univ of California Press; 1961

[94] Gilman S. Accounting Concepts of Profit. New York, NY: Ronald Press Company; 1956

[95] Gordon MJ. Scope and method of theory and research in the measurement of income and wealth. The Accounting Review. 1960;**35**(4):603

[96] Kelley AC. Can corporate incomes Be scientifically ascertained? The Accounting Review. 1951;**26**(3):289-298

[97] Kuter M, Baker CR, Gurskaya M. Profit calculation in a late 14th century sole proprietorship: The case of rancesco Datini. Accounting Historians Journal. 2022;**49**(1):15-28

[98] Lee TA. Income and Value Measurement: Theory and Practice. 3rd ed. New York, NY: Chapman Hall; 1994

[99] Littleton AC. Concepts of income underlying accounting. The Accounting Review. 1937;**12**(1):13-22

[100] Report of Study Group on Business Income. Changing Concepts of Business Income. Houston, TX: Scholars Book Co.; 1975 (Originally published on 1952)

[101] Saito S, Fukui Y. Whither the concept of income? Accounting, Economics, and Law: A Convivium. 2019;**9**(1):1-16

[102] Schmidt F. Is appreciation profit? Accounting Review. 1931;**6**(4):289-293

[103] Solomons D. Economic and accounting concepts of income. The Accounting Review. 1961;**36**(3):374-383

[104] Sterling R. Theory of Measurement of Enterprise Income. TX: Scholars Book Co; 1970

[105] Thuronyi V. The concept of income. Tax Law Review. 1990;**46**:45

[106] Al-Adeem KR, Alhasan H. An empirical investigation on the understandability of accounting income. Journal of Accounting and Finance. 2023;**23**(3):35-54

[107] Beaver WH, Demski JS. The nature of income measurement. Accounting Review. 1979;**54**(1):38-46

[108] Bedford NM. Income Determination Theory: An Accounting Framework. Reading, Mass: Addison-Wesley Pub Co; 1965

[109] Al-Adeem KR. Sustaining mutual and market interests in the auditor and corporate client relationship. In Refereed Proceeding of the American Accounting Association Mid-Atlantic Region Meeting. April 23-25, 2015. 2015. Available from: http://aaahq.org/Portals/0/documents/misc/Mid-Atlantic%202015%20Proceedings%20up%20to%20p217.pdf

[110] Al-Adeem KR. Auditing Corporate Reports and Financial Statements Externally: Truth or Mirage. International Journal of Financial, Administrative and Economic Sciences. [InArabic] 2024a;**3**(3):32-64

[111] Al-Adeem KR. Corporate Governing in Appearance: An Unintended Consequence of Governing Corporations. Working Paper. Riyadh, Saudi Arabia: King Saud University; [In Arabic] 2024b

[112] Al-Adeem KR. The historical and Islamic roots of the double-entry bookkeeping system. –academic for. Social Science. 2024c;**2**(1):21-52 [In Arabic]

[113] Aveh FK, Awunyo-Vitor D, Afriyie RO. Independence, objectivity and integrity compliance by public sector internal auditors in Ghana: Evidence from Ashanti region. International Journal of Critical Accounting. 2016;**8**(5-6):444-462

[114] Bazerman MH, Morgan K, Loewenstein GF. The impossibility of auditor independence. Sloan Management Review. 1997;**38**(4):89-94

[115] Bazerman MH, Loewenstein G & Moore DA. Why Good Accountants Do Bad Audits. Harvard Business Review. 2002. Retrieved on 27 June 2023. Available from: https://hbr.org/2002/11/why-good-accountants-do-bad-audits

[116] Bazerman MH, Moore DA. Is it time for auditor independence yet? Accounting, Organizations and Society. 2011;**36**(4-5):310-312

[117] Belkaoui AR. The New Context of the Accounting Profession. 2017. Available at SSRN: https://ssrn.com/abstract=3037598 or doi:10.2139/ssrn.3037598

[118] Bost TG. The Sarbanes-Oxley Act of 2002: A Summary. 7, (4). D.C, Washington: National Legal Center for The Public Interest; 2003

[119] Brehmer Thomas. Sarbanes-Oxley Fails on Auditor Independence. Accounting Today. 2013. Retrieved on 6 November, 2020. Available from: https://www.researchgate.net/publication/327835966 An_Analysis_of_the_Relationship_between_Audit_Fees_and_Non-audit_Fees_thlyl_allaqt_byn_atab_almrajt_watab_alkhdmat_alastsharyt_alakhry

[120] DeZoort FT, Taylor MH. Commentary- public interest view of auditor independence: Moving toward auditor reliability when considering and promoting audit quality. Accounting and the Public Interest. 2015;**15**(1):53-63

[121] DeZoort FT, Holt T, Taylor MH. A test of the auditor reliability framework using lenders' judgments. Accounting, Organizations and Society. 2012;**37**(8):519-533

[122] Green DA. Whither and whether auditor independence. Gonzaga Law Review. 2008;**44**(3):365-410

[123] Kleinman G, Palmon D. Understanding Auditor-Client Relationships: A Multi-Faceted Analysis. Princeton, NJ: Markus Wiener Publishers; 2001

[124] Kleinman G, Anandarajan A, Palmon D. Who's to judge: Understanding issues of auditor independence versus judicial independence. Accounting, Economics and Law: A Convivium. 2012;**2**(1):1-50

[125] Livne G. Threats to auditor independence and possible remedies. Q-Finance. 2013:1-13

[126] Loewenstein G, Moore DA, Bazerman MH. Enron failures show U.S. auditing system is in dire need of big change. Pittsburgh Post-Gazette. 2002;**January 15**:11–C

[127] Mautz RK, Sharaf H. The Philosophy of Auditing. Sarasota, FL: American Accounting Association; 1961/2006

[128] McKenna F. Five Auditor Independence Issues PCAOB SAG Not Yet Addressed. Re: The Auditors. 28 June 2023. 2013. Available from: http://retheauditors.com/2013/11/11/five-auditor-independence-issues-pcaob-sag-not-yet-addressing/

[129] Murnighan JK, Bazerman MH. A perspective on negotiation research in accounting and auditing. The Accounting Review. 1990;**65**(3):642-657

[130] Nouri H, Lombardi D. Auditors' independence: An analysis of Montgomery's auditing textbooks in the 20th century. Accounting Historians Journal. 2009;**36**(1):81-112

[131] O'Connor SM. The Inevitability of Enron and the Impossibility of 'auditor independence' under the Current Audit System (March 1). 2002. Available at SSRN: https://ssrn.com/abstract=303181

[132] Reiter SA, Williams PF. The philosophy and rhetoric of auditor independence concepts. Business Ethics Quarterly. 2004;**14**(3):355-376

[133] Shockley RA. Perceptions of auditors' independence: An empirical analysis. The Accounting Review, LVI. 1981;**4**:785-800

[134] Taylor MH, DeZoort FT, Munn E, Thomas MW. A proposed framework emphasizing auditor reliability over auditor independence. Accounting Horizons. 2003;**17**(3):257-266

[135] Tinker A, Sy A. Politicisation of the professions. International Journal of Economics and Accounting. 2017;**8**(1):61-66

[136] Turnbull S. How can auditors lie about being independent? Keeping Good Companies. 2006;**58**(10):584

[137] Beattie V, Fearnley S, Brandt R. Behind Closed Doors. New York, NY: Palgrave; 2001

[138] Fontaine R. An Empirical Study of Canadian Companies to Determine the Client's Perspective on their Preferred Relational Approach with their Financial Auditor. (Unpublished Ph. D. dissertation). Montréal, Canada: Université du Québec; 2010

[139] Previts GJ. The Scope of CPA Services a Study of the Development of the Concept of Independence and the Profession's Role in Society. Ronald Press; 1985

[140] Al-Adeem KR. Reconceptualizing the management–auditor relationship by appling the general partnership contract to challenge independence: Ideals ersus reality. Journal of Accounting, Business and Management (JABM). 2022a;**29**(1):155-193

[141] Baldacchino PJ. The auditor–management relationship in a microstate perspective. Master of philosophy (MPhil) dissertation written for the Loughborough University. 1992

[142] Capital Market Authority (CMA). Corporate Governance Regulations. Saudi Arabia; 2006

[143] Capital Market Authority (CMA). Corporate Governance Regulations. Amendment Saudi Arabia; 2009

[144] Capital Market Authority (CMA). Corporate Governance Regulations. Saudi Arabia; 2015

[145] Capital Market Authority (CMA). Corporate Governance Regulations. Saudi Arabia; 2017. Available from: https://cma.org.sa/en/RulesRegulations/Regulations/Documents/CGRegulations_en.pdf

[146] Capital Market Authority (CMA). (2018). Corporate Governance Regulations. Amendment Saudi Arabia. Available from: https://cma.org.sa/en/MediaCenter/PR/Pages/CGRAmendments.aspx

[147] Capital Market Authority (CMA). (2023). Corporate Governance Regulations. Amendment Saudi Arabia. Available from: https://cma.org.sa/RulesRegulations/Regulations/Documents/CorpGovReg.pdf

[148] Adelopo I. Auditor Independence: Auditing, Corporate Governance, and Market Confidence. London, UK: Gower Publishing Limited; 2012

[149] Sanchez MH, Agoglis CP, Hatfield RC. The effect of auditors' use of

reciprocity-based strategy on auditor – client negotiations. The Accounting Review. 2007;**83**(1):241-263

[150] Al-Adeem KR, Al-Sogair I. Effectiveness of the board of directors in monitoring executive management: Preliminary evidence from Saudi Arabia. Journal of Governance and Regulation. 2019;**8**(3):72-82

[151] Schneider A, Church BK, Ely KM. Non-audit services and auditor independence: A review of the literature. Journal of Accounting Literature. 2006;**25**:169

[152] Berle AA, Means GC. The Modern Corporation and Private Property. New York: Macmillan; 1932

[153] Al-Hazzani MM, Al-Adeem KR. Do corporations' annual reports address shareholders as proprietors? Evidence from Saudi Arabia. International journal of Auditing and Accounting Studies. 2020;**2**(2):175-192

[154] Merino BD. An analysis of the development of accounting knowledge: A pragmatic approach. Accounting, Organizations and Society. 1993;**18**(2-3):163-185

[155] Al-Adeem K. Dear investors: I Am good at what I am for, accounting says. Austin Journal of Accounting, Audit and Finance Management. 2003c;**3**(1):1006

[156] Jensen MC, Meckling WH. Theory of the firm: Managerial behavior, agency costs and ownership structure. Journal of Financial Economics. 1976;**3**(4):305-360

[157] Fogarty T, Magnan ML, Markarian G, Bohdjalian S. Inside agency: The rise and fall of Nortel. Journal of Business Ethics. 2009;**84**(2):165-187

[158] Baskin JB, Maranti PJ Jr. A History of Corporate Finance. Cambridge University Press; 1997

[159] Hendriksen ES, Breda M. Accounting Theory. New York: McGraw-Hill; 2001

[160] Hunt HG III, Hogler RL. Agency theory as ideology: A comparative analysis based on critical legal theory and radical accounting. Accounting, Organizations and Society. 1990;**15**(5):437-454

[161] AdbulaHakam AYA. Analyzing Fundamental of Positive Accounting Theory and its Role in Building Standards and Selecting among Alternatives: Analysis and Application. Sudan: Master Thesis University of Um Dorman; 2008

[162] Alameen BI. Accounting choices from positive accounting theory perspective. Accounting. 1997;**4**(12):44-48 Sects. (in Arabic)

[163] Alkhadash HM. Directions of accounting research in Jordanian peer-reviewed journals. Almanarah. 2004;**10**(2):289-313 (in Arabic)

[164] Almotairi OS. Contemporary directions in accounting research. Accounting. 1997;**4**(12):36-39 (in Arabic)

[165] Almotairy OS, Motwali TA. Contemporary research approaches (interpretive and critical) and their absence from Arabian accounting research. Arabian Accounting Journal. 2002;**5**(1):1-37 (in Arabic)

[166] Alshamam MAH, Abdula Alhafez AMK. Influence of directions of accounting research during the period 1926-2019 on constructing accounting theory. LFU (French-Lebanese University). 2020;**5**(1):713-745 (in Arabic)

[167] Hassan NT. Determines of accounting choices in Saudi public

companies. Egyptian Accounting Review. 2014;**4**(8):73-107 (in Arabic)

[168] Ibraheem AAM. Accounting Theory. (in Arabic). 2002

[169] Ibraheem AAM. Evaluating traditional and modern research approaches in contracting accounting theory. Contemporary Commercial Research Journal. 2008;**22**(1):50-85 (in Arabic)

[170] Jazar MMA. Directions of accounting research published in journals in Saudi Arabia during the period 2001-2017. Public Administration Journal. 2019;**57**(3):529-548 (in Arabic)

[171] Othamn AI. Evaluating the scientific methodology for the conceptual framework of positive accounting theory. Public Administration. 2000;**39**(4):729-772 (In Arabic)

[172] Reiter SA. Economic imperialism and the crisis in financial accounting research. Critical Perspectives on Accounting. 1998;**9**(2):143-171. DOI: 10.1006/cpac.1997.0120

[173] Saraj MA. Analysis of the effectiveness of using normative approach and positive approach in accounting theorization. Public Administration. 1989;**63**(1):143-176 (in Arabic)

[174] Jeanjean T, Ramirez C. Back to the origins of positive theories: A contribution to an analysis of paradigm changes in accounting research. Accounting in Europe. 2009;**6**(1):107-126. DOI: 10.1080/17449480902 896510,Sects.107-126

[175] Volkova ON. Accounting as an Academic Discipline: Paradigmatic Limits and Research Programs, (December 1). 2018. Availabel from: https://ssrn.com/abstract=3294658

[176] Al-Adeem KR. The impact of the emergence of accounting from practice and practical application on the development of accounting theory. Journal of Accounting, Saudi Accounting Association. 2011;**53**:15

[177] Anonymous, Harper T. License to Steal: The Secret World of Wall Street and the Systematic Plundering of the American Investor. New York, NY: HarperBusiness; 1999

[178] Sikka P, Stittle J. Debunking the myth of shareholder ownership of companies: Some implications for corporate governance and financial reporting. Critical Perspectives on Accounting. 2019;**63**:1-14

[179] Berendon A. The Number: How the Derive for Quarterly Earnings Corrupted Wall Street and Corporate American. New York, NY: Random House; 2003

[180] Tapscott D, Ticoll D. The Naked Corporation: How the Age of Transparency Will Revolutionize Business. New York, NY: free Press; 2003

[181] Bricker R, Chandar N. Where Berle and Means went wrong: A reassessment of capital market agency and financial reporting. Accounting, Organizations and Society. 2000;**25**(6):529-554

[182] Roe MJ. Strong Managers, Weak Owners: The Political Roots of American Corporate Finance. Princeton, NJ: Princeton University Press; 1994

[183] Bebchuk LA. The myth of the shareholder franchise. Va. L. Rev. 2007;**93**:675-732

[184] Chabrak N. The shareholder value mythology and the market "communion". Law and Financial Markets Review. 2014;**8**(1):27-38

[185] Chu J. Filling a nonexistent gap: Benefit corporations and the myth

of shareholder wealth maximization. Southern California Interdisciplinary Law Journal. 2012;**22**:155

[186] Clark T. Deconstructing the mythology of shareholder value: A comment on Lynn Stout's "the shareholder value myth". Accounting, Economics and Law. 2013;**3**(1):15-42

[187] Dent GW Jr. The essential unity of shareholders and the myth of investor short-termism. Delaware Journal of Corporate Law. 2010;**35**:97

[188] Ho K. In the name of shareholder value: Origin myths of corporations and their ongoing implications. Seattle University Law Review. 2019;**43**:609-930

[189] Ireland P. Company law and the myth of shareholder ownership. The Modern Law Review. 1999;**62**:32

[190] Knafo S, Dutta SJ. The myth of the shareholder revolution and the financialization of the firm. Review of International Political Economy. 2020;**27**(3):476-499

[191] Macey J. Sublime myths: An essay in honor of the shareholder value myth and the tooth fairy. Texas Law Review. 2013;**91**:911-924

[192] Mukwiri J. Myth of shareholder primacy in English law. European Business Law Review. 2013;**24**(2):217-241

[193] Stevelman F. Myths about shareholder value. Accounting Economics and Law: A Convivium. 2013;**3**(1):1-14. DOI: 10.1515/ael-2013-0005

[194] Stout LA. The mythical benefits of shareholder control. Virginia Law Review. 2007:789-809

[195] Stout LA. The Shareholder Value Myth: How Putting Shareholders First Harms Investors, Corporations, and the Public. Berrett-Koehler Publishers; 2012a

[196] Stout LA. New thinking on" shareholder primacy". Accounting, Economics, and Law. 2012b;**2**(2)

[197] Weinstein O. The shareholder model of the corporation, between mythology and reality. Accounting, Economics and Law. 2013;**3**(1):43-60

[198] Schrempf-Stirling J. The shareholder value myth: How putting shareholders first harms investors, corporations, and the public by Lynn A. Stout. Bus Ethics Q. 2013:486-489

[199] Fogarty TJ. Circle 'round' the wagons: Sarbanes Oxley and impression management. In: The American Accounting Association (AAA) Annual Meetings, Honolulu, August. 2003

[200] Fontaine R, Pilote C. Practical summary: Clients' preferred relationship approach with their financial statement auditor. Current Issues in Auditing. 2012;**6**(1):P1-P6

[201] Anandarajan A, Kleinman G, Palmon D. Auditor independence revisited: The effects of SOX on auditor independence. International Journal of Disclosure and Governance. 2008;**5**(2):112-125

[202] Chung H, Kallapur S. Client importance, nonaudit services, and abnormal accruals. The Accounting Review. 2003;**78**(4):931-955

[203] Cheney G. USA come in the from cold. Australian CPA. Melbourne: December. 2002;**72**(11):30

[204] Cottell PG, Perlin TM. Accounting Ethics. Connecticut NY: Quorum Books; 1990

[205] Adams RB, Ferreira D. Strong managers, weak boards? CESifo Economic Studies. 2009;**55**(3-4):482-514

[206] Cohen JR, Hayes C, Krishnamoorthy G, Monroe GS, Wright AM. The effectiveness of SOX regulation: An interview study of corporate directors. Behavioral Research in Accounting. 2013;**25**(1):61-87

[207] Fama EF, Jensen MC. Separation of ownership and control. The Journal of Law and Economics. 1983;**26**(2):301-325

[208] Brown JR Jr. Criticizing the critics: Sarbanes-Oxley and quack corporate governance. Marquette Law Review. 2006;**90**:309

[209] Dubnick MJ. Sarbanes-Oxley and the search for accountable corporate governance. GovNet ejournal. 2007:140-172

[210] Parles L, O'Sullivan SA, Shannon JH. Sarbanes-Oxley: An overview of current issues and concerns. Review of Business. 2007;**27**(3):38-46

[211] Shakespeare C. Sarbanes-Oxley act of 2002 give years on: What have we learned. Journal of Business & Technology Law. 2008;**3**:333-350

[212] Alkhafaji AF. Corporate governance: The evolution of the Sarbanes-Oxley act and its impact on corporate America. Competitiveness Review: An International Business Journal. 2007;**17**(3):193-202

[213] Guerra JE. The Sarbanes-Oxley act and evolution of corporate governance. The CPA Journal. 2004;**74**(3):14-15

[214] Mitchell LE. The Sarbanes-Oxley act and the reinvention of corporate governance. Villanova Law Review. 2003;**48**:1189-1216

[215] Valenti A. The Sarbanes-Oxley act of 2002: Has it brought about changes in the boards of large US corporations? Journal of Business Ethics. 2008;**81**:401-412

[216] Petra ST, Loukatos G. The Sarbanes-Oxley act of 2002: A five-year retrospective. Corporate Governance: The International Journal of Business in Society. 2009;**9**(2):120-132

[217] Ray DM. Corporate boards and corporate democracy. Journal of Corporate Citizenship. 2005;**20**: 93-105

[218] Willits SD, Nicholls C. Is the sarbanes-oxley act working? The CPA Journal. 2014;**84**(4):38

[219] Brickley JA, Zimmerman JL. Corporate governance myths: Comments on Armstrong, Guay, and weber. Journal of Accounting and Economics. 2010;**50**(2-3):235-245

[220] Sonnenfeld J. Good governance and the misleading myths of bad metrics. Academy of Management Perspectives. 2004;**18**(1):108-113

[221] Chomsky N. Profit over People: Neoliberalism & Global Order. Seven Stories Press; 1999

[222] Clark T. Mechanisms of corporate rule. In: Mander J, Goldsmith E, editors. The Case against the Global Economy and for a Turn toward the Local. San Francisco, CA: Sierra Club Books; 1996. pp. 295-308

[223] Smith BM. A History of the Global Stock Market: From Ancient Rome to Silicon Valley. University of Chicago Press; 2004

[224] Davis GF. Managed by the Markets: How Finance Re-Shaped America. OUP Oxford; 2009

[225] Briloff AJ. Old myths and new realities in accountancy. The Accounting Review. 1966;**41**(3):484-495

[226] Monti-Belkaoui, J., & Riahi-Belkaoui, A. (1996). Fairness in Accounting.

[227] Rudkin K. Accounting as myth maker. Australasian Accounting, Business and Finance Journal. 2007;**1**(2):13-24

[228] Thompson G. Is accounting rhetorical? Methodology, Luca Pacioli and printing. Accounting, Organizations and Society. 1991;**16**(5-6):572-599

[229] Praeger Morgan G. Accounting as reality construction: Towards a new epistemology for accounting practice. Accounting, Organizations and Society. 1988;**13**(5):477-485

[230] Mouck T. Institutional reality, financial reporting and the rules of the game. Accounting, Organizations and Society. 2004;**29**(5-6):525-541

[231] White GI, Sondhi AA, Fried D. The Analysis and the Use of Financial Statements (3rd ed.). Hoboken, NJ: John Wiley & Sons, Inc. 2003

[232] Bayou ME, Reinstein A, Williams PF. To tell the truth: A discussion of issues concerning truth and ethics in accounting. Accounting, Organizations and Society. 2011;**36**(2):109-124

[233] Briloff AJ. The Truth about Corporate Accounting. Harpercollins; 1981

[234] Conway RA. The Truth about Public Accounting: Understanding and Managing the Risks the Auditors Bring to the Audit. Independently published; 2020

[235] MacNeal K. Truth in Accounting. University of Pennsylvania Press; 1939

[236] Lee TA. The FASB and accounting for economic reality. Accounting and the Public Interest. 2006a;**6**(1):1-21

[237] Lee TA. Reply to Contemprory—Cunning plans, spinners, and ideologues: Blackadder and Baldrick try accounting for economic reality. Accounting and the Public Interest. 2006b;**6**(1):45-50

[238] Lee TA. The ontology and epistemology of social reality in accounting according to Mattessich. Accounting and the Public Interest. 2009;**9**(1):65-72

[239] Macintosh NB. COMMENTARY—Accounting—Truth, lies, or "bullshit"? A philosophical investigation. Accounting and the Public Interest. 2006a;**6**(1):22-36

[240] Macintosh NB. Commentary: The FASB and accounting for economic reality: Accounting–truth, lies, or "bullshit": A philosophical investigation. Accounting and the Public Interest. 2006b;**6**(2006):22-36

[241] Mattessich RV. FASB and social reality—An alternate realist view. Accounting and the Public Interest. 2009;**9**(1):39-64

[242] Williams PF. COMMENTARY—Accounting for economic reality: Whose reality, which justice? Accounting and the Public Interest. 2006;**6**(1):37-44

[243] Chambers RJ, Wolnizer PW. A true and fair view of position and results: The historical background. Accounting Business and Financial History. 1991;**1**(2):197-213

[244] Cowan TK. Are truth and fairness generally acceptable? The Accounting Review. 1965;**40**(4):788

[245] Hines RD. Financial accounting: in communicating reality, we construct reality. Accounting, Organizations and Society. 1988b;**13**(3):251-261

[246] Houghton KA. True and fair view: An empirical study of connotative meaning. Accounting, Organizations and Society. 1987;**12**(2):143-152

[247] Kirk N. Perceptions of the true and fair view concept: An empirical investigation. Abacus. 2006;**42**(2):205-235

[248] Macintosh NB, Shearer T, Thornton DB, Welker M. Accounting as simulacrum and hyperreality: Perspectives on income and capital. Accounting, Organizations and Society. 2000;**25**(1):13-50

[249] Mattessich R. Reality and Accounting: Ontological Explorations in the Economic and Social Sciences. Newyork, NY: Routledge; 2013

[250] McKernan JF, Kosmala K. Doing the truth: Religion–deconstruction–justice, and accounting. Accounting, Auditing & Accountability Journal. 2007;**20**(5):729-746

[251] Nahapiet J. The rhetoric and reality of an accounting change: A study of resource allocation. Accounting, Organizations and Society. 1988;**13**(4):333-358

[252] Parker RH, Wolnizer PW, Nobes C, editors. Readings in True and Fair. Taylor & Francis; 1996

[253] Williams SJ. Assets in accounting: Reality lost. Accounting Historians Journal. 2003b;**30**(2):133-174

[254] Elkhashen EM, Ntim CG. Accounting and philosophy: The construction of social reality framework. Journal of Accounting and Taxation, Forthcoming. 2018

[255] Hines RD. The FASB's conceptual framework, financial accounting and the maintenance of the social world. Accounting, Organizations and Society. 1991;**16**(4):313-331

[256] Sterling R. Accounting power. Journal of Accountancy. 1973

[257] Mouritsen ML, Mano RM. Professor STERLING was correct IN 1973: When WILL we ever learn? Journal of Accounting & Finance Research. 2005;**13**(2):59-65

[258] Belkaoui A. The Coming Crisis in Accounting. Westport, Connecticut: Quorum Books; 1989

[259] Levitt A Jr. The numbers game. The. CPA Journal. 1998;**68**(12):14

[260] Brewster M. Unaccountable: How the Accounting Profession Forfeited a Public Trust. John Wiley & Sons; 2003

[261] Costanza-Chock S, Raji ID, Buolamwini J. Who audits the auditors? Recommendations from a field scan of the algorithmic auditing ecosystem. In: Proceedings of the 2022 ACM Conference on Fairness, Accountability, and Transparency. 2022. pp. 1571-1583

[262] Levitt A Jr. Who audits the auditors? The New York Times. 2002;**151**(52001):A2-A2

[263] Loomis CJ. Lies, damned lies, and managed earnings. Fortune, 02, August. 1999. pg. 74-92

[264] Brearey DC, Al-Adeem KR. Thinking beyond the black box: Sterling shows accountants the way toward relevance. Journal of Finance and Accountancy. 2019;**2019**

[265] Jensen M, Meckling WH. The nature of man. Journal of Applied Corporate Finance. 1994;**7**(2):4-19

[266] Al-Adeem KR. Need to understand human nature and the nature of fraud in our attempts to discover it. General Accounting Court Journal (the Official Journal of the General Court for Accounting in Saudi Arabia). 2022c;**3**(1):100-130

[267] Antle R. Auditor independence. Journal of Accounting Research, Spring. 1984;**22**(1):1-20

[268] Bayou ME, Reinstein A. A systemic view of fraud explaining its strategies, anatomy and process. Critical Perspectives on Accounting. 2001;**12**(4):383-403

[269] Sanchez. I Know that Fraud Will be an Issue in Everything I Do in the Future. 2002. Available from: https://www.chicagotribune.com/news/ct-xpm-2002-10-02-0210020276-story.html

[270] DeFond ML, Wong TJ, Li S. The impact of improved auditor independence on audit market concentration in China. Journal of Accounting and Economics. 2000;**28**:269-305

[271] Rogowska B. Ethical aspects of normative theories of accounting. Annales. Etyka w Życiu Gospodarczym. 2018;**21**(8):17-29

[272] Berry MH. Doctoral research. The Accounting Historians Journal. 1983;**10**(1):137-148

[273] Al-Adeem KR. Deepening the Understanding in the Conceptual (Theoretical) Framework for Financial Accounting. Saudi Arabia: King Saudi University Press; 2020a [In Arabic]

[274] Al-Adeem KR. Cultural challenges for countries implementing international financial reporting standards without contributing to their creation. African Journal of Accounting, Auditing and Finance. 2020b;**7**(1):66-86

[275] Anderson JA. The potential impact of knowledge of market efficiency on the legal liability of auditors. The Accounting Review. 1977;**52**(2):417-426

[276] Belkaoui. The Cultural Shaping of Accounting. CT, Westport: Quorum Books; 1995

[277] Boedker C, Chua WF. Accounting as an affective technology: A study of circulation, agency and entrancement. Accounting, Organizations and Society. 2013;**38**(4):245-267

[278] Burchell S, Clubb C, Hopwood A, Hughes J, Nahapiet J. The roles of accounting in organizations and society. Accounting, Organizations and Society. 1980;**5**(1):5-27

[279] Chambers RJ. Accounting-"one of the finest inventions of the human spirit". Contemporary Accounting Research. 1984;**1**(1):1-22

[280] Chambers RJ. The conditions of research and accounting. Journal of Accountancy. 1960;**June**:33-38

[281] Cowan TK. A pragmatic approach to accounting theory. The Accounting Review. 1968;**43**(1):94-100

[282] Scott DR. Conservatism in inventory valuations. Papers and proceedings of tenth annual meeting of the American Accounting Association of university instructors of accounting. The Accounting Review. 1926;**1**(1):18-30

[283] Hatfield HR. Historical defense of bookkeeping. Journal of Accountancy. 1924;**37**(4):241-253

[284] Hopwood AG. On trying to study accounting in the contexts in which it operates. Accounting, Organizations and Society. 1983;**8**(1/2):278-305

[285] Lehman G. A critical perspective on the harmonization of accounting in a global world. Critical Perspectives on Accounting. 2005;**16**(7):975-992

[286] Littleton AC. Accounting Evolution to 1900. The Academy of Accounting Historians. Accounting History Classical Series; 1966/1981

[287] Vatter WJ. Postulates and principles. Journal of Accounting Research. Autumn. 1963;**1**(2):179-197

[288] Yamey BS. Notes on the origin of double-entry bookkeeping. The Accounting Review. 1947;**22**(3):263-272

[289] Nelson EG. Science and accounting. The Accounting Review. 1949;**24**(4):354-359